IMES
Institute of Middle East Studies
معهد دراسات الشرق الأوسط

THE MISSIOLOGY BEHIND THE STORY

Voices from the Arab World

EDITED BY Jonathan Andrews

This book is a unique window into missions in the Middle East in recent history. While no such overview can do justice to the last two hundred years, the contributors have carefully tried to cover as much as possible in a fair and balanced perspective. This book will be especially useful for evangelical Westerners who want to get an idea of what God has done and is doing in the Middle East today and the cultural and political contexts in which Christian ministry takes place. It is important to note that much more than is written in the book is taking place, as the author clearly acknowledges, and also that particularly in Egypt a great part of the work is being done through the Coptic Orthodox Church which is not mentioned in this overview.

Ramez Atallah
General Director,
The Bible Society of Egypt

At a time when there is so much conflict in the Middle East and so many doubts about the survival of Christianity, we need to know that there are many Christians who are rooted there and actively engaged in their communities in creative and imaginative ways. These are powerful stories – the majority told by nationals – not only about subjects you would expect from evangelical Christians, like church planting and discipleship, but about peace-making, inter-faith dialogue and social justice. As the title suggests, we are told not only *what* these Christians are doing but *why* they are doing it. Perhaps we are seeing here a fresh fulfilment of Isaiah's promise about 'a new thing' that God might be doing before our eyes.

Colin Chapman
Former Lecturer in Islamic Studies,
Near East School of Theology, Beirut, Lebanon
Visiting Lecturer,
Arab Baptist Theological Seminary, Beirut, Lebanon

If we thought little is happening among Arabs, we need to think again. *The Missiology behind the Story* clearly demonstrates that the God of mission has a church in the region that is reaching out in numerous ways. As expected, evangelism, church planting and discipleship are part of that mission, but so are relief and development, justice, peacebuilding and more. Moreover, through case studies in each of the ten chapters, it is very encouraging to see the involvement by Muslim background believers that is helping to change every aspect of life and society. And this is only the tip of the iceberg. Much of what is going on cannot be written about publicly for security reasons. Finally, what is most heartening for me is that increasingly people throughout the Arab world are being given an opportunity to respond to the question Jesus asked his own disciples: "Who do you think I am?" Truly, God is at work among the 313 million Arabic speakers in our world, and we can look forward to even greater things to come.

Warren Larson, PhD
Senior Research Fellow and Professor,
Zwemer Center for Muslim Studies,
Columbia International University, South Carolina, USA

This is a sensitive and broad introduction to Christian worship and witness in the birthplace and heartlands of the three major monotheistic religions of the world – Judaism, Christianity, and Islam. Against the backdrop of the history of the region and the transfer of leadership from expatriate to national leaders, it takes the reader through helpful descriptions of evangelism, church planting, discipleship, relief and development, social justice, dialogue, peace-building, media, children and youth, and leadership formation – all described by a variety of workers. If you only can have one book on the these topics, this is the book to get.

J. Dudley Woodberry, PhD
Dean Emeritus and Sr. Professor of Islamic Studies,
Fuller Theological Seminary, Pasadena, California, USA

Institute of Middle East Studies Series

The Missiology behind the Story

Langham

GLOBAL LIBRARY

The Missiology behind the Story

Voices from the Arab World

Edited by

Jonathan Andrews

GLOBAL LIBRARY

© 2019 The Arab Baptist Theological Seminary (ABTS)

Published 2019 by Langham Global Library
An imprint of Langham Publishing
www.langhampublishing.org

Langham Publishing and its imprints are a ministry of Langham Partnership

Langham Partnership
PO Box 296, Carlisle, Cumbria, CA3 9WZ, UK
www.langham.org

ISBNs:
978-1-78368-598-1 Print
978-1-78368-599-8 ePub
978-1-78368-600-1 Mobi
978-1-78368-601-8 PDF

British Library Cataloguing-in-Publication Data
A catalogue record for this book is available from the British Library

ISBN: 978-1-78368-598-1

Cover & Book Design: projectluz.com
Cover image: © Lotharingia - stock.adobe.com

To the memory of those from the Middle East and elsewhere who have pioneered Christian mission in the region and to the glory of the name of Jesus.

CONTENTS

Foreword

The vision for *The Missiology behind the Story* was born over five years ago, in 2013, in the course of a conversation between the Arab Baptist Theological Seminary (ABTS) and some of our international partners. It was pointed out to us that ABTS was having a significant influence in informing the thinking of many around the world about the nature and diversity of the church's mission in our world today. ABTS's Institute of Middle East Studies has held an annual conference/consultation since 2004, addressing the church's role in the mission of God both in the Middle East North Africa (MENA) region and globally. This annual gathering of over a hundred evangelicals from all around the world has gradually become a flagship event for ABTS. It has informed and transformed both our thinking and practice, and many of our global partners tell us that it has been doing the same for them. The past fifteen years in the aftermath of 9/11 have been defining the global church's thinking about Islam, the Middle East, Christian-Muslim relations, people displacement, conflict and war. The church in the MENA region has not stood idle. It has engaged in mission, witness, discipleship, interfaith dialogue, peacebuilding, Bible translation, youth work, relief and development, and many other ministries. But it is often the case that when the people of God are deep at work in the mission of God, they do not have time to step back, reflect, write, and influence others who are further away from the frontlines. We began the journey of putting together *The Missiology behind the Story* to address this very gap. We do not claim to be either comprehensive or unique. Many other faithful followers of Jesus are engaged in outstanding work for the kingdom. This book is a collection of unique voices in conversation and partnership from the MENA region that we hope will be heard and engaged with far beyond the region.

As expected, though this project is a humble beginning, the sheer intent of bringing together sufficient diversity of experiences and ministries was in itself a very ambitious endeavour. This explains why it took so many years to bring these chapters together. As the reader will note, the countries covered by the stories and reflections related in this book are far from comprehensive of the entire MENA region. Nor are all valid topics covered. For example, the original book outline planned to include chapters on the missional church, publishing, creation care, and Bible translation. But for practical reasons, we were not able to address these. These omissions – and no doubt several others – are due to our own limitations rather than because we view them as of lesser importance.

The book was originally to be co-edited by two theologians from the Majority World. But for the very reasons mentioned above, primarily "overbusyness" at the frontline of ministry, this was not achieved and was a cause for further delays. In the end, we decided to hand the editorial process to the very able hands of a professional writer with an outstanding familiarity with the region's challenges and realities, and it is with deep gratefulness that we extend our appreciation to Jonathan Andrews. He worked tirelessly and with great dedication towards the fulfilment of a messy and unfinished task, bringing it to fruition in record time. Without Jonathan, disparate stories and missiological reflections would still be lingering in our computer files. ABTS is overwhelmed with feelings both of humility and pride in the final outcome, and we give praise to the Lord God for the opportunity to take our voice out in engagement with Christ's church everywhere, as we engage together as the universal church in sharpening our thinking and practice in obedience to his calling and invitation into his mission in the world.

Martin Accad
Beirut, Lebanon
February 2019

Acknowledgements

I wish to express my appreciation for the thoughtfulness of each contributor. I have sensed the feeling and passion at the root of their involvement. I trust they are comfortable with how their contributions have been moulded into what I trust is a coherent whole.

This book has been a challenge to bring together. Mission is such a broad subject, and there are numerous aspects to several topics. This diversity shapes several chapters. For example, the missiological reflection in chapter 8 focuses on online aspects of media, albeit not exclusively.

The greatest source of challenge has been the context of the Middle East itself. So much of what is being done by Christians as part of *missio Dei* is discreet; publicity is shunned. Those leading some activities are convinced that inappropriate descriptions of their work will lead to serious issues with the authorities; such fears are well founded. I trust that Christians throughout the region will approve of how their area of work has been described.

This same observation explains why readers might regard some chapters as less than comprehensive. For example, chapter 10 on leadership development focuses almost exclusively on seminary or college-based programmes. This omits the much less formal, but arguably more widely used, use of correspondence-based courses. What is prudent to say about such matters? Perhaps, that the increasing use of online methods by formal programmes is drawing diverse strands closer together.

I wish to thank Elie Haddad for the invitation to act as the Editor for this book. My thanks also to Vivian Doub of Langham Publishing and Elias Ghazal who has acted as my liaison with the ABTS and IMES (see abbreviations). My thanks to Jesse Wheeler for mentoring Samah Fakhreldein as she compiled many of the case studies and for overseeing the development of many of the background sections. I personally am indebted to Malcolm Catto, David Hunt, Gordon Grüneberg and Alison Pascoe who have read drafts of the book and scrutinized the detail. Their support and expertise is invaluable.

Finally, my thanks to Wendy, my wife, for her steadfast support.

Jonathan Andrews
January 2019

Abbreviations

ABTS	Arab Baptist Theological Seminary, located in Mansourieh, Beirut, Lebanon
AUB	American University of Beirut, Lebanon
AWGMCD	The Arab Working Group on Muslim-Christian Dialogue, Lebanon
BBC	Bethlehem Bible College
CEOSS	Coptic Evangelical Organization for Social Services, Egypt
CMS	Church Mission Society, formerly called the Church Missionary Society
DBS	Discovery Bible Study
DESA	United Nations Department of Economic and Social Affairs
DMAH	Dar Manhal al Hayat, Lebanon
ETSC	Evangelical Seminary in Cairo, Egypt
FEBA	Far East Broadcasting Association
IFD	Inter-Faith Dialogue
IMES	Institute of Middle East Studies, based at ABTS (see above)
ISIS	Islamic State in Iraq and Syria (see glossary)
JETS	Jordan Evangelical Theological Seminary, located in Amman, Jordan
KDEC	Kasr Dobara Evangelical Church, Cairo, Egypt
LSESD	Lebanese Society for Educational and Social Development
MECC	Middle East Council of Churches
MENA	Middle East and North Africa
NGO	Non-Governmental Organization
UBS	United Bible Societies
UN	United Nations
UNDP	United Nations Development Programme

USA	United States of America
UK	United Kingdom
YFC	Youth for Christ

Introduction

How is God at work in the Middle East and North Africa (MENA) in the twenty-first century?

God established his church in this region in the first century. It has endured to this day, initially as marginalized and persecuted, then as mainstream, even dominant (at least religiously) before becoming marginalized again. In this century, it knows both acceptance and persecution in different parts of this diverse region.

This century has seen dramatic changes in many places across the region. The more obvious ones are linked to violent conflict, others to the removal of long-standing rulers including former President Mubarak of Egypt. Also significant is the effect of changes in technology; the global online social media era is profoundly affecting the region.

How are Christians across the Middle East responding to such changes? One recurring theme is that new opportunities have emerged for the church to express its faith and hope in Jesus, to be agents of transformation in local communities and to share the good news of Jesus with the ever-rising numbers willing to listen. These are exciting times for those willing to look beyond the news headlines to see what God is doing.

This book demonstrates that the God of mission has a church in the world, encapsulated by the phrase *missio Dei*. God is the initiator of mission, it is his idea; we act in obedience to him. Jesus is our primary example. On the evening of his resurrection he appeared to his first followers and said, "As the Father has sent me, so I am sending you" (John 20:21). "Sending" is a theme running through John's Gospel (e.g. John 1:6; 3:16–17 and 16:7), a motif that climaxes with Jesus, sent by his heavenly Father, sending his followers. Jesus gives us a mandate and a model for mission, for *missio Dei*.

What is mission? What does it comprise? This book describes ten types of activities that Middle Eastern Christians undertake as an expression of their faith in Jesus. Some aspects are almost universally accepted by Christians of all traditions, for example, teaching Christianity to the next generation and the training of church leaders. Other aspects are undertaken by many, including sharing the good news of Jesus with non-Christians, although some are more discreet about doing so than others. Some aspects are contentious, for example, Muslim-Christian dialogue. It is argued here that in the context of parts of the Middle East, such dialogue is an inescapable activity for

Christians. Consequently, within the evangelical Christian circles globally, Middle Eastern Christians are at the forefront of such activity, providing an example that the church worldwide should examine and apply to their own contexts. Historically, the church throughout the Middle East has gained much from missional activity by others; in this area it is also contributing to the church elsewhere.

Whereas Christian mission in previous centuries was frequently characterized by the expression "the West to the rest," in the twenty-first century it is encapsulated by "from everywhere to everywhere." The MENA region is no exception to this development within global Christianity.

One observation is that much missional activity was initiated by Westerners. One theme of the twentieth century was the move to the institutions and organizations they formed, adapting and becoming led by indigenous people. Another theme running through this book is how more Arab Christians started similar activities and organizations. One emerging trend in the twenty-first century is the increasing involvement of those from Muslim backgrounds in *missio Dei*, of Christ's followers acting according to his mandate and model among their peers. This can be viewed as the fulfilment of the agenda that the Westerners came with many decades before: they sought to teach Muslims the good news of Jesus; but, finding very little response, became involved in supporting Christians. One unintended consequence in some places was that they exacerbated tensions amongst Christian denominations.

One theme in this book is who is seen by whom as "us" and "them": examples include Christians and Muslims, and evangelicals and other Christians. Such dynamics have changed over time and this century has seen further adaptations. Recent developments can be seen as both a result of *missio Dei* – Christ breaks down barriers – and as an enabler of Christian engagement in society.

The general pattern is that each chapter has three elements. We start with some background material, often a historical survey of the subject. The central section comprises several case studies, based on an interview with a key participant with much of the material presented using their words, or their words translated into English. The third section is a missiological reflection which describes the biblical mandate for this area of missional activity. In a few chapters, I, as editor, have added a reflection based on my years working in support of Christian communities throughout the MENA region. These are primarily intended for Western and other non-Middle Eastern readers, encouraging us to be discerning in how we stand alongside our brothers and sisters in this volatile, diverse and fascinating region. The material may be of relevance in other contexts, which I regard as another gift of God given to the global church through the Christians of the Middle East. I have also inserted some sentences introducing the next section and some cross-referencing to other chapters. These additions are in italic type so as to make it clear whose voice we are hearing.

The book might divide activity into neat chapters. However, real life is not as straightforward: many areas overlap and interact with others. So, the first three chapters on evangelism, church planting and discipleship interact with one another. Subsequent chapters include aspects of these subjects within their focus on a different topic. For example, chapter 8 on media includes elements of explaining Jesus's life and teaching to non-Christians, supporting isolated small groups of new Christians and passing on the faith to the next generation, elements that can be labelled evangelism, church planting and discipleship.

Many of the contributors (see contributors' bios) and those interviewed for the case studies refer to historical events which have profoundly shaped them and their situation. Some things are referred to several times, for example, the Lebanese Civil War, typically dated 1975 to 1991. The appendix consolidates such material; it provides an overview of the history underlying the context of today. Readers with limited knowledge of the Middle East might find it helpful to read this before proceeding into chapter 1.

Likewise, many sections of the book refer to the growing numbers of people choosing to follow Jesus having been raised as adherents of another faith. The terminology applied to such people varies, including "believers from Muslim backgrounds," "choosing to follow Jesus" and "converts." All have their strengths but also their limitations and unfortunate connotations in some settings.

One aspect that rapidly becomes apparent is that most of the case studies are taken from Lebanon and Egypt. Why? One reason is that Christian activity in these countries can be discussed more openly than elsewhere. One trend prevalent throughout the region is that society welcomes the results of the humanitarian and development aspects of Christian mission. One example is the number of schools, universities and hospitals founded by missionaries which endure to this day. It is perhaps paradoxical that some such actions are not always officially recognized or appreciated when initiated. Consequently, some of those involved operate with great discretion, and most endeavour to carefully manage publicity about their work. This makes some Christian mission work inappropriate content for a public medium such as this book. As you read what follows, be aware that in many places throughout the Middle East, North Africa and the Arabian Peninsula – the Arab world (see glossary) –

many of Christ's followers are acting in similar ways, but less publicly, playing their part in *missio Dei*.

So, to our first chapter on making the good news of Jesus known.

1

Evangelism in the Mission of God

By Samar Khoury, with Donnie Bentley and Samah Fakhreldein (see contributors' bios).

A Brief Survey of Western Protestant Missions to the Middle East and North Africa 1850–1950 (by Donnie Bentley)

Protestant missionary efforts to the Middle East and North Africa by the 1850s and 1860s had developed into a variety of ministries and institutions. Concerted and coordinated effort by major Protestant missions like the American Board, the Presbyterian Mission and the Church Mission Society (CMS) continued until World War One during which the Ottoman Empire collapsed. Mission efforts by many denominations were then scaled back, and their presence and influence decreased. Although other missionary organizations would become involved, the missionary presence by the 1950s was only a shadow of what it had been during the second half of the nineteenth century. Missionaries had initially sought the evangelization of Jews and then Muslims, but ended up working primarily with indigenous Christians of all traditions in an effort to bring Protestant revival. Though they would eventually establish their own denominations, converts from Islam were few. However, the impact of Protestant institutions on society was significant, and their legacy continues to this day.

The German missionary historian Julius Richter wrote in 1910 that "The great Protestant Missions have been sent to the Near East [sic] with the earnest desire, not to found new churches but by self-denying service and by the introduction of Protestant vitality, to prepare the way for reform from within."[1] Protestant missionaries initially encouraged converts to attend the nearest church, and their aim was that the ancient churches would be "awakened" and then reach Muslims.[2] However, this hope for Protestant reformation from within was not to be realized. Protestants viewed the ancient churches as venerable but decaying and were not about to accept the Monophysite or "Nestorian" (see glossary) theological positions of Coptic and Assyrian Christians or the veneration of icons and the Virgin Mary of the Orthodox and Maronite churches.[3] Roman Catholic missionary influence had already been established for centuries with groups like the Maronites; their Patriarch quickly decreed that he would excommunicate members who rented homes to Protestants and proclaimed a curse on anyone that visited or hosted them.[4] Protestants faced the responsibility of caring for and shepherding a small number of people that had been attracted to Protestantism. Many were assistants and language tutors.

In 1850 Protestants sought and obtained recognition as an official community from the Ottoman authorities. This granted them the protection and relative freedoms of the *millet* system (see glossary).[5] Legal authority provided legitimacy for Protestant institutions, and these soon began to flourish. In 1856 the Sultan was pressured by France and England to institute reforms and declared that "Every distinction or designation tending to make any class whatever of the subjects . . . inferior to another class, on account of their religion, language or race, shall be forever effaced from the administrative protocol . . . all forms of religion are and shall be freely professed in my dominions."[6] The Protestant missions viewed this as an open invitation to expand their work. Rev C. G. Pfander's translation of his *The Balance of Truth* into Turkish in 1864, which included polemic attacks on the character of the prophet Mohammad, seems to have been a turning point, and the liberal policy

---

1. Julius Richter, *A History of Protestant Missions in the Near East* (Edinburgh: Oliphant, Anderson & Ferrier, 1910), 70.

2. Habib Badr, "Evangelical Churches and Missions in the Middle East: Lebanon, Syria and Turkey," in *Christianity: A History of the Middle East* (Beirut: MECC, 2005), 714.

3. The use of icons within several Christian traditions is often misunderstood by others. Just as with computer operating systems, icons are a way into something; so icons within Christian worship are a route to God. They are valuable for what they represent, not for any intrinsic value of their own. The artistic element in icons is also seen in stained glass and other features of church buildings in all Christian traditions.

4. Richter, *History of Protestant Missions*, 188.

5. Badr, "Evangelical Churches," 714. See also Jonathan Andrews, *Identity Crisis: Religious Registration in the Middle East* (Malton: Gilead Books, 2016).

6. Richter, *History of Protestant Missions*, 172.

of the Ottomans was then reversed. The biggest blow to Protestant efforts was the decree that Muslim students were prohibited from attending Protestant schools.[7]

Despite these difficulties, schools for boys and girls continued to be founded and were attended by Christians who were attracted to, and willing to pay for, the Western education that the Protestants were offering. This attendance often continued even as Eastern churches began offering their own schools for free to their members. By the 1900s women outnumbered men on missionary rosters, and education efforts provided a good platform for ministry.[8] By the late 1940s concerted efforts to eliminate illiteracy were being carried out. Some schools were nationalized after the end of colonial rule, and others followed the worldwide trend of secularization, like the American University of Beirut (founded as the Syrian Protestant College) and the American University in Cairo. However, there are many Protestant schools that continue their ministries to this day.

Printing presses and publishing houses were another concerted ministry effort of the Protestant missionaries. Eli Smith and Cornelius Van Dyck spent a total of eight years each in collaboration with Butros Bustany and the al-Azhar graduate Sheikh Yusif Asir to produce an Arabic translation of the Bible. By 1910, 1,250,000 bound copies had been distributed, and the Van Dyck version is still used in the majority of Protestant churches around the Middle East.[9] This publication eventually led Catholics to reverse their stance against laity possessing the Scriptures, and they produced their own translation which closely followed the Protestant one. Orthodox schools under Russian patronage obtained Bibles and schoolbooks directly from the Protestant printing press. In Egypt, 1860 was declared as "The Year of the Bible." The missionaries bought the Nile boat *Ibis*, and Rev McCage accompanied by four Egyptians rode through Assyut on horseback shouting, "The Bible for Sale."[10] The Nile Mission Press of Cairo would eventually ship books and pamphlets as far as China, South Africa and Venezuela.[11] In Beirut, the Protestant printing presses were used to aid the Arab renaissance of literature.

Initially, mission efforts tended to be centralized within a few large mission boards. The Anglican CMS partnered with the Prussian King Frederick William

---

7. Richter, 77.

8. Charles E. Farhadian, *Introducing World Christianity* (Oxford: Blackwell, 2012), 17.

9. Richter, *History of Protestant Missions*, 215.

10. Adib Naguib Salamah, "Evangelical Missions and Churches in the Middle East: Egypt and Sudan," in *Christianity: A History of the Middle East* (Beirut: MECC, 2005), 737.

11. Farhadian, *Introducing World Christianity*, 17.

IV in Palestine. The CMS also had a significant presence in Egypt, and a few outposts in Sudan as well as one in Baghdad, Iraq. The American Board of Commissioners for Foreign Missions concentrated their efforts in Lebanon, with a few stations in Syria and Iraq. The Presbyterian missionaries worked in Egypt, Lebanon, Syria and parts of Iraq. The mission scene had expanded and changed by 1914 as there were Pentecostals in Egypt, Methodists in Algeria, Reformed Church of America missionaries in Oman and Quakers in Lebanon.[12] Muslim converts were few with estimates of about two hundred for Egypt and a similar number for Morocco in 1950. Protestant missionaries started ministry outreaches among Iranian Shi'ite pilgrims to Iraq, Jews in Palestine, Alawites in Syria, and the Druze (see glossary) in the mountains of Lebanon. The Druze were at one point ready to convert to Christianity en masse in order to avoid conscription into the Sultan's army, but American Board missionaries objected to this based upon their Western individualistic understanding of salvation.[13] Apostasy laws were another limitation on conversion, and missionaries pressed the issue of religious liberty with the League of Nations and the United Nations. They supported the Universal Declaration of Human Rights in 1948, notably that Article 18 explicitly includes the right to religious conversion.[14]

Indigenous Christians faced periods of severe persecution during this era of missions, and Protestant missionaries were involved in providing aid and shelter. During the conflict between Maronites and Druze in 1845 in Deir El-Qamar, Lebanon, Protestant missionaries fed, sheltered and secured the safe passage for hundreds of Maronites.[15] In turn the Greek Orthodox and Maronite bishops of Beirut offered proclamations that similar protection was to be offered to American Mission members should they suffer a similar calamity. Ludwig Schneller founded an orphanage in Jerusalem for Maronites (see glossary) orphaned during massacres in Damascus during 1860. The Armenian genocide (see glossary) led the Protestant missionaries to establish more official churches as a part of their humanitarian response. Relations between Protestant and Armenian churches became cordial to the point that national pastors would exchange pulpits.[16]

In the second half of the nineteenth century in cities such as Cairo and Beirut that had a significant presence of traditional Christians, Protestants

---

12. Farhadian, 17.

13. Richter, *History of Protestant Missions*, 193.

14. Farhadian, *Introducing World Christianity*, 17.

15. Richter, *History of Protestant Missions*, 192.

16. Richter, 69.

were able to form home Bible-study groups that would eventually develop into established churches. The missionaries then expanded their efforts and established outposts in hundreds of villages throughout the Middle East. From Beirut, missionaries travelled up into the mountain villages. From Cairo, they travelled up the Nile establishing mission outposts in Sudan. Medical outposts were established in a few port cities in the Gulf. There were a variety of outreaches including schools, publishing houses, hospitals, churches, seminaries and even a mental health hospital. In impoverished communities these efforts were received very positively even if there was resistance to Protestant theology. Political turmoil and a lack of converts would take a toll on many of these outposts, and in countries like Lebanon they would eventually be consolidated back into city centres such as Tripoli, Sidon, Beirut and Zahle.

One of the biggest challenges for Protestant mission during this era was that it was firmly and unequivocally identified with the West. By 1910, half of the communicants in congregations in Beirut and Tripoli had emigrated to the West.[17] Missionaries followed colonial trade routes and would appeal to their ambassadors when they ran into trouble. They often viewed the spreading of Western civilization as synonymous with the spread of Christianity. There was a mentality of spiritual conquest and crusade. The prevalent eschatological position of the day was post-millennialism. Missionaries came to establish the kingdom of God on earth where poverty and the social and physical ills of society would be addressed through concerted Christian effort. This modernist confidence and optimism were quickly met with a series of setbacks and defeats. The veteran missionaries that stayed and persevered, like Samuel Zwemer, developed new approaches that were less focused on Christendom and more attentive to making Christ known within the Muslim community. Western education and medical missions addressed strongly felt needs in the communities that the missionaries worked in, so it was natural that these efforts continued to flourish and spread.

Case Studies (by Samah Fakhreldein)

We move our focus to more recent times. Our case studies describe some evangelistic endeavours from the 1990s onwards. We might ask what happened between 1950 and 1990. In summary, these trends continued and other areas of mission began, the details of

---

17. Richter, 224.

which are included in subsequent chapters. For now, we will visit Egypt, Syria and Lebanon.

A Visionary in a Foreign Land

Pastor Jamal Makkar is an Egyptian leader who began his ministry with Life Agape Egypt during the 1990s. He felt called at that time to train leaders for ministry so he moved to Jordan to equip eighteen leaders for full-time ministry and mission in Middle Eastern countries. The training primarily focused on how to undertake evangelism by using different approaches and then following-up and discipling those who chose to follow Jesus's call. Soon, Jamal married Micheline, a Lebanese leader who shared his heart for ministry, and together they felt called to serve in Syria. All the doors for ministry in Syria were closed before them except for one local church which opened its doors to them and their ministry. So, in spite of the security challenges – for example, evangelism is forbidden outside church walls – and a lack of encouragement from the local church, Jamal and Micheline moved to Syria in 1996. They started from this one church and went on to train eight leaders in how to share the gospel, follow-up and disciple new believers, and send others out in mission. Within two years, their group had grown to include one hundred-fifty disciples.

Jamal and Micheline started to undertake direct evangelism in Christian and mixed areas. They trained teams in evangelism including practical assignments. They taught participants to respect the beliefs of others while also proclaiming the essence of Christianity without fear of consequences. They respected cultural differences and followed the traditions of each village and city they visited. God used them to share the gospel with the Druze community, a group of whom started their own home church in 2006. This Druze church grew to include almost seven hundred members.

At that time in Syria it was forbidden to talk about Christianity outside of church buildings. In response, Jamal and his team thought creatively about how they might take the gospel outside of the walls of the church. One approach was to project the *Jesus Film* (see glossary) onto the outer walls of the church building. This allowed the public to learn the real story of Jesus's crucifixion. However, this indirect form of evangelism resulted in many security officers coming to question them about their ministry. Jamal stated that "I saw the hand of the almighty Lord present every time I was called in for questioning." In dealing with the authorities in other matters, he was aware that "Whenever I applied for any approval from the authorities or from the Ministry of Culture,

God performed miracles, and I received approval in a very short amount of time."

During the 2000s, Life Agape produced a movie called *Damascus Speaks* about the life and ministry of the Apostle Paul. As the launch date approached, they sent a copy to President Assad of Syria to tell him that a terrorist came to Damascus and became a saint. The president liked the movie and insisted that its premiere be held in the national opera house and all the expenses be covered by the presidency. Approximately eight thousand people attended the premiere, many of whom were not Christians. They heard the gospel of Jesus presented in a clear and direct way by the movie. This event was protected by the authorities and a representative from the presidency attended.

Nevertheless, the ministry of Life Agape in Syria has many challenges from both inside the Christian community as well as from the outside. Within the Christian community the youth suffer from a lack of role models, and a generation gap has developed between the youth and elders in the church. This has given the youth who grew up in the churches a negative impression of God and his people. In addition, the emigration of Christians from the region, especially as a result of the crisis that erupted in 2011, has left many churches without leaders. From the outside, the challenge comes from the security services and the political authorities.

A Prayer Warrior

Karen is young, yet behind her beautiful face lies a stubborn prayer warrior, a Lebanese woman with the heart and courage for serving Palestinian refugees. She began her ministry at an aid kitchen feeding refugees in need. Over time, this ministry grew to include home visits and sharing the gospel. Later on, Karen became part of a service organization catering to university students. Her initial student group quickly grew as she was able to meet and share the gospel with many young students. Her vision for ministry is to reach all the youth in the various universities, sharing with them the gospel, training them in leadership and supporting them as they establish their own ministries where they can worship the Lord within their particular contexts.

In addition, Karen has been part of a worship team which goes into Beirut's night club district every Saturday night. Their aim is to be the light of the Lord in these dark places, singing worship songs, distributing the Bible or evangelistic tracts and speaking with those who visit the clubs. Many young people have been attracted to them and to their worship, spending hours talking about God, atheism, agnosticism, homosexuality and other issues that the youth long to discuss. When asked about her reasons behind this approach, she responded, "When I first followed Jesus, I came from these dark places. Therefore, I promised the Lord that I would remain faithful and never forget where I came from. I have a continual passion for saving people like myself from Satan's hands. While reading Acts 26:17–18, God put in my heart the love and a calling for addicts, homosexuals and prostitutes. The pastor of my church blessed this ministry and encouraged us to move forward."

Karen's group has faced many challenges. They have faced harassment for being a group of young women who stay out late at night among "the drunks." In addition, one of her main challenges has been the need for workers and partners in her ministry, a difficult ministry requiring long-term commitment.

One of the stories Karen shared with regard to her work in the clubs was of how God has protected her and her team in the midst of a variety of difficult situations. For example, one night they were walking around the area and praying for people when a group of men who were clearly drunk began going around sexually harassing young women. When passing by Karen's group, they suddenly stopped talking until the group left, after which they resumed speaking inappropriately to young women on the streets.

Sometimes Karen's group feels desperate when days pass and no one responds to their evangelistic outreach, but even in the midst of this despair they feel God is renewing their hope and encouraging them. As Karen says, "It is not an easy ministry. The unreached people we often work with can be difficult and the girls know that; however, we also know that we are doing our part in building the kingdom of God."

Kasr Dobara Evangelical Church Caravans

Kasr Dobara Evangelical Church's (KDEC) caravans travel from village to village throughout poorer areas in Egypt. Whether hot, cold or rainy, they continue to focus on their evangelistic mission in both word and deed. These caravans visit villages where no church buildings exist nearby, inviting Christians from churches of all traditions to pray and praise together in one united meeting.

Part of the ministry of the caravans is to pray with those who are sick or in need of financial support as well as to distribute relief boxes and required medications, as prescribed by a doctor. Each group always includes a medical doctor, "prayer warriors" for healing and the casting out of demons, and preachers of the gospel. Their primary approach to evangelization is through holding revival meetings, visiting people in their homes, praying with them, speaking about salvation in Jesus and inviting them to attend revival meetings held during evenings. Sometimes they are rejected by Christians who attend churches of other traditions. Sometimes they are rejected by those upon whose doors they knock. They might be harassed or spat upon while walking in villages, but they just shake it off and move on.

Ehab, a servant who has dedicated his life to this ministry, shares a story about one of his caravan trips:

> Once, I was leading the caravan in one of the poorer villages in Upper Egypt. On the first night, I prepared myself for preaching. When I started to pray for the topic, my soul suddenly became disturbed within me, and the name of a man, "Ashraf," came to my mind. I do not know this person, so I asked myself why this name is repeating continuously through my mind. I began to pray for this Ashraf and asked a friend to preach instead of me. This repeated for the second and third day. On the fourth day, the team went out to do home visits and I remained behind. While I was alone, someone came and asked me to visit his brother's house because his brother had been sick for many days. I went with him and found a young man who was very sick. When I asked him his name, he told me "Ashraf." I began to cry, and I got down on my knees to pray that he might be healed. I told him about what the Spirit had done within me for the past three nights just for him. That very day, he prayed for salvation and began to follow Jesus.

Missiological Reflection: Indigenous Christians in *Missio Dei* (by Samar Khoury)

So, what would get a young, newly-married couple, Jamal and Micheline, to move out of both their countries of origins into a third country, and a country that restricts Christian activities? What would drive a group of young ladies every week into the dark streets of Beirut where they might be harassed by drunkards? In all of the stories narrated above, we see how individuals of different backgrounds and nationalities are going outside their comfort zones and being immersed into daily adventures that are not empty of challenges and obstacles in order to serve and reach out to others who are very different from them.

This is exactly the gospel that we have received, good news of reconciliation and goodwill towards all the nations, even the nations with whom our countries might have shared a bad history. For it is a mission that goes beyond the political and historical narrative and transcends it to a divine narrative of unconditional love. We remember the words of Paul in Galatians 3:28, "There is neither Jew nor Gentile, neither slave nor free, nor is there male and female, for you are all one in Christ Jesus."

Great efforts were made for many years by the Protestant missionaries to reach out to the people of the Middle East. This has been the trend of many Christian missionaries throughout the centuries who faced all kinds of troubles and struggles in response to the greatest mission of all, when the Son of God left his glory to come to our broken world. He lived among us, was clothed with the culture of his time, healed our sick, carried our sins and gave us long-lasting peace with him. It is the example of Jesus that still fuels us today to take his love and message to the people who have not yet received it.

What great examples of faithful Christians we have above. The Makkar family lived neither in Lebanon nor in Egypt, but instead made Syria their home. Karen, who is Lebanese, sensed a calling to reach out to the Palestinians and the young people in the dark parts of her city, and the KDEC caravans go to the poorest of the poor and the sick in Upper Egypt. It is sad to hear that in addition to their service and sacrificial giving, they still experience rejection, questioning and harassment. But it is beautiful to see that in spite of the challenges they faced, their ministries were fruitful, and we can tell how their faith matured throughout the years as they were overwhelmed by God's provision and guidance. For instance, we see that especially when brother Ehab breaks down in tears when he finally meets Ashraf or when Karen and the girls are surprised to see the guys who were harassing other girls just go past them without uttering a word. The rejection and the persecution only remind us of the whole reason why Jesus came to our world in the first place. Jesus himself was harassed because of the company he chose to be seen with, and people said of him, "Here is a glutton and a drunkard, a friend of tax collectors and sinners" (Matt 11:19). We are blessed to have such a Saviour, who says: "Blessed are you when people insult you, persecute you and falsely say all kinds of evil against you because of me. Rejoice and be glad, because great is your reward in heaven, for in the same way they persecuted the prophets who were before you" (Matt 5:11–12).

It is beautiful to see how the carriers of the good news find solutions to every obstacle by using the creativity that God has given them to overcome the challenges they face. Kasr Dobara Church, for instance, used caravans that could take the gospel to places that are unreached; it is very unlikely that the people they are reaching out to will one day walk into Kasr Dobara's church building. They cannot come to us, so we go to them. This reflects the daily life of Jesus who used to go from one village to another and visit people in their homes. Many of the miracles and the teachings happened on the way to someone's house or inside of it. From observing the life of Jesus and the experience of many of us in the field, we can confidently say that the most effective evangelism is the one we do outside the church walls. The young men and women that Karen reaches out to would probably not find it interesting to go to a church service, and so Karen and her team, as a small church body, carry the gospel to the streets. We hear the creative idea of Pastor Jamal when he projected the *Jesus Film* on the outer walls of the church building, in a country where proclaiming the good news of Jesus in public is prohibited. So, again we see how these Christians put their lives and comfort on the line for the sake of making Jesus known to the same people who might end up persecuting them.

It is amazing to see how Pastor Jamal ends up sharing the good news boldly without defying or disrespecting the authorities. It is incredible to hear the story of how he visited the president, presented the movie of Paul's conversion to him, and was granted permission by him to show it, and as a result, eight thousand people, many of them non-Christians, watched it. This boldness comes from the assurance of the faith that we have. We know who eventually holds the highest authority because Jesus said: "All authority in heaven and on earth has been given to me. Therefore go . . . " (Matt 28:18–19). The disciples who saw the risen Christ could not be quiet about it; they could not contain it. The same goes for us today. After we have witnessed the power of the resurrected Christ as he transforms our lives day by day, how can we be quiet about it?! There is definitely a risk being taken when we reach out to those who are high in authority, but at the same time it is extremely strategic as you can gain their respect when they see your boldness and confidence in your faith. This might have repercussions on thousands of people as we observed above. We are reminded of how the solid faith of Daniel had a great impact on King Darius in chapter 6 of the book of Daniel and earlier on King Nebuchadnezzar. The demonstration of God's power in saving Daniel prompted King Darius to issue a decree to his whole empire that urged them to fear and honour the God of Daniel for "His kingdom will not be destroyed, his dominion will never end. He rescues and he saves; he performs signs and wonders in the heavens and on the earth" (Dan 6:26–27).

Throughout this chapter, we see how the acts of love that accompanied the gospel of love allow it to reach people more successfully. The KDEC caravans, for instance, were welcomed in the various villages because local Christians saw the needs of their neighbours, had compassion on them, and gave them a hand to help them through their pain, whether through offering medical care, food portions, or prayer for healing and liberation, as well as declaring the gospel clearly in revival meetings. This holistic approach reminds us of the ways of our Lord in dealing with people as whole beings and not just addressing merely the spiritual or the physical realms. He obviously expects us to follow his footsteps: "For I was hungry and you gave me something to eat, I was thirsty and you gave me something to drink, I was a stranger and you invited me in, I needed clothes and you clothed me, I was ill and you looked after me, I was in prison and you came to visit me" (Matt 25:35–36).

The Protestant missions to the Middle East succeeded vastly in following these words, and it is crucial at this point to reflect on the various approaches of the Protestant missions to the Middle East and see what lessons we can learn from their successes and their setbacks. Starting with the successes of these mission projects, it is admirable to see the massive number of institutions that have been formed to serve the people of the region. It is also impressive to see how practical they were in their projects. They saw the need and poured out the human and the financial resources accordingly. The legacy today is so many schools, hospitals, churches, printing presses, seminaries, orphanages and mental health facilities. Their work in the poor villages helped them gain favour in spite of the theological differences that they shared with the historic churches. Moreover, we see how they gained the trust of the Maronites and the Armenians when they provided shelter and aid for their people in those times when these people were being persecuted. On the other hand, they were still seen as "the West" which is not easily welcomed by Middle Easterners who had had enough colonization over the years. Moreover, the fact that some missionaries considered spreading the Western civilization as equal to spreading the kingdom of God in the Middle East was never the best approach since it removes the people they are reaching from their unique cultural identity. It is impressive to notice how the Makkars, on the other hand, were careful to respect the cultural traditions wherever they carried the unchangeable gospel even within the Arab world. Therefore, it is important to take the cultural identity into consideration when carrying out any evangelistic missions.

We have to give credit to the Protestant missionaries who tried to do the reformation from within the pre-existing churches and did not originally aim to start new churches. Alas, this was not communicated clearly to the local churches. Even now, many historic Christians call evangelicals "sheep-stealers," and some of the bad reputation that developed in the past remains today. It is a relief that now Western missions focus more on making Christ known to the

Muslim community and are not approaching the long-standing non-Protestant Christians as they did before.

Another approach that I really appreciate is the one done by Kasr Dobara Church that was described in our third case study. They go to the villages that do not have a local church building and invite Christians of all traditions to join together in prayer and worship. Therefore, they do not threaten the existence of any local church, but instead go to the marginalized and unreached. This initiative implies respect and acknowledgment of the other party. It shows that we should focus as different Christian denominations on what unites us, instead of focusing on what divides us. Moreover, such initiatives indirectly trigger the traditional churches to become more active and effective in their own contexts.

With time, evangelicals in Lebanon are gaining more trust and favour from the historic churches as they focus their missional actions with non-Christian communities, rather than seeking to reform the historic churches, as they continue to faithfully carry out the mission of love in words and actions to their neighbours. We also notice how we are beginning to see the fruits of the Protestant missions more clearly in the past few decades, since now the task is being carried out by the locals who are able to preserve the cultural identity of recipients while sticking to biblical principles.

This is why there is a big need to train indigenous leaders in order that they would minister within their local contexts. This has been the key to the spread of Christianity throughout the ages and across cultures for, if evangelism is not coupled with ministry training, the gospel cannot be carried out from one generation to another. The very first thing that Jesus did at the beginning of his ministry was calling young men to walk alongside him, observe his life, listen to his teaching and practise what they learned in the nearby villages and towns.

The Syrian crisis has brought many of us new neighbours who are of a different cultural and religious background. We have discovered that the most strategic approach is that of training Syrians in ministry and sending them to minister to their own people. Moreover, the need for more leaders is crucial if we want to see the youth of today restored to healthy relationships with God. The words of Pastor Jamal and those of Karen emphasize the dire need for young leaders who will be an anchor in faith for the youth to look up to and be inspired by. Therefore, we can learn from both of these examples of leaders to pour out our lives and resources into young Christ-followers who would carry out the good news in their own circles of friends, where our feet cannot reach. Therefore, let us be on the lookout for potential leaders and live out the words of Paul in 2 Timothy 2:2, "And the things you have heard me say in the presence of many witnesses entrust to reliable people who will also be qualified to teach others." (*We will look at this further in chapter 10.*)

It is truly a privilege to learn from the experiences of these brothers and sisters as well as from the history of Protestant missions to the Middle East. The church can learn a lot from the journeys of those whose efforts have produced so many benefits that we still see in our society today, and surely, we learn from the unsuccessful approaches and ministry attempts. In spite of the failures, the obstacles and the persecution that faces evangelists, nothing seems to drown the overwhelming joy we feel when sharing the love of Christ with another person. It just reminds me of these words from Jeremiah 20:9, "But if I say, 'I will not mention his word or speak any more in his name,' his word is in my heart like a fire, a fire shut up in my bones. I am weary of holding it in; indeed, I cannot." The same God is alive today who, in the New Testament, sent Philip to explain the Scriptures to the Ethiopian (Acts 8:26–39) and the same one who urged Ananias to go and pray for Saul in order to have his eyes opened and get him ready to carry his gospel to the Gentiles (Acts 9:10–19). He is a God who still designs divine appointments today, like the beautiful encounter between Ehab and Ashraf, in order to call many people to follow him and then send them out to carry his gospel and reach out to other "lost sheep" wherever they may have wandered.

To God be all the glory.

2

Church Planting in the Mission of God

We follow consideration of evangelism by looking at where new followers of Christ will worship. Some will be able to join existing churches, others will require the establishment of new churches, a process known as church planting. We note that all churches were founded, or planted, at some point. Many have been involved in establishing further churches, often to accommodate additional members or to provide new places of Christian worship as urban centres expand.

Our considerations are provided by Mary (not her real name) assisted by Donnie Bentley and Samah Fakhreldein with additional material provided by the editor. Mary uses the story of the church where her husband is the priest to illustrate various aspects of church planting.

Background: A Dynamic Process
(by Donnie Bentley and Jonathan Andrews)

Church planting in the Middle East and North Africa takes various forms and occurs within a wide diversity of contexts. It is influenced by Muslim majority societies, extended family cohesion, and the significance of tribal and sectarian identity. Legal permission to plant churches or not varies from country to country, and in some countries varies in practice from place to place, typically between urban and rural settings. Even in countries where Arab Christians are freely allowed to worship and operate church buildings, these same freedoms are almost never extended to those from Muslim backgrounds.

This has naturally led to different church planting approaches. The political and social turmoil in many countries since 2011 has created new church planting opportunities, and new types of church have emerged. Conversely, many church buildings have been attacked or closed because of persecution or displacement. The region is diverse and dynamic; so too is church planting.

All Christians are members of the "one holy, catholic and apostolic church" to use the formulation of an historic creed. Many followers of Christ belong to a local church, rooted in a geographic location. In this chapter we are discussing the establishment of local churches in response to the emergence of a group of disciples of Jesus in a particular location.

Understanding of what we mean by a church – a local church – can vary as illustrated by Algeria and Morocco, neighbouring North African countries.

In Algeria, a church is defined by the following elements. There is a leadership team of three people and a programme of events throughout the week with a gathering for worship on one day. Usually this will be on Friday, the main day of worship throughout the country. A fellowship is something less than this, such as one leader and few if any events other than a gathering for worship or a Bible study. The hope is that fellowships start as a few people meet to read the Bible and pray together. Over time, as others join them, the other elements that define a church are put in place, and the fellowship becomes a church.

In contrast, in neighbouring Morocco, a church is any gathering of three or more nationals who have chosen to follow Jesus.

Church planting in this sense is very diverse. We can use David Garrison's *A Wind in the House of Islam* as the basis of an illustration. The chapter on the Arab world includes a description of a church planting movement in an unnamed country in the Middle East.[1] After the book was published, this network of churches went through a very difficult period; one could say that it collapsed. The leader was severely harassed by the authorities and moved to a nearby country where he restarted his activities of evangelism and establishing small, house-based churches for those who decide to follow Jesus. Back in his home country, new leaders – plural – emerged who regenerated what he had started, strengthened it and, under the Holy Spirit's direction, the network grew in number and depth of understanding of Jesus.

How people who become followers of Jesus from non-Christian backgrounds participate in church is largely determined by their local context: what is possible in each location. One analysis describes three broad categories.

---

1. David Garrison, *A Wind in the House of Islam* (Monument: WigTake, 2014), 201–220.

In summary, first, those willing and able to join legally recognized churches and become part of Christian communities. These people become Christians in the social sense as well as religiously. Second, those who differentiate themselves from other Muslims but do not become members of a church or part of Christian communities. Effectively, they become a new social-religious grouping. Third, those that consciously remain part of Muslim communities in order to speak about Jesus. Typically, they avoid outward symbols of Christianity which might hinder their witness. In particular, whilst they would meet regularly for prayer, fellowship and Bible study, they would avoid establishing anything that could be perceived to be a church building.[2]

Case Studies (by Samah Fakhreldein)

Our case studies take us from Lebanon to Egypt and back to Lebanon.

Planting a Church, Planting Lifetime Friendship

Ahmad described his family's history.

> The story started almost eighty years ago, when my grandfather had a dream of a man dressed in white Bedouin clothes who told him how unhappy he was with his lifestyle. The man in the dream advised my grandfather to go to Jerusalem where he would meet another man who would show him the truth. My grandfather believed this might have been the Lord Jesus himself. There in Jerusalem he met with a missionary called Ibrahim in a miraculous way. Ibrahim explained the good news of Jesus, and my grandfather became a follower of Jesus. Subsequently, when the politics of the area changed, the Bedouins had to settle somewhere else. My family settled near the Assi River in Lebanon, and the missionary Ibrahim came all the way from Palestine to visit my tribe bringing a friend of his, Fouad, a Bible distributor. When Fouad and Ibrahim came to visit the tribe, my grandfather would invite everyone to come and meet in the big tent and listen. They would stay for two or three days, reading, explaining the Bible, and sharing the life of the Bedouins. In this way, the whole

---

2. Jonathan Andrews, *Last Resort: Migration and the Middle East* (Malton: Gilead Books, 2017), 351–355.

family was discipled together. My grandfather sent as many young people as he could to schools founded by missionaries in Palestine, Syria and Lebanon so that they would get an education and learn about Jesus.

Today, Ahmad is part of an organic community of followers of Jesus that can be described as a home church in the large sense of the term. It was established many years ago; he is the third generation of believers in this church. The community has been supported by several others since then.

Some of Fouad's family cared spiritually for this community for many years. They did discipleship training, and for a long time a woman from his family taught stories from the Bible to the children at one of the schools established by the Bedouin tribe. With time, she became part of the Bedouin family, as she has a very strong friendship bond with everyone. She continues to study the Bible with many of the women. Several younger people from the tribe are growing as leaders and serving with her in the ministry of discipleship.

Since 2012, this ministry has expanded to include relief for Syrian families who came to the neighbourhood seeking refuge from the war in Syria. The dedication of the Bedouin family to serve Syrian people motivated the family to respond to the needs of the displaced. They were supported by several charitable organizations in these endeavours. God's love motivates his followers to help others. (*We will return to this subject in chapter 4.*)

Sameh is an Egyptian Christian who assisted this ministry from 2014 to 2017. He said that, "as a house church, we endeavour to express the hope that Christ brings to this community, many of whom have lost a lot and are in need of friendship." Sameh's focus was to share the love of Jesus and his Word through relief and children's ministry. The group grew in number as more families became involved in discipleship meetings. Many homes became open for hosting the meetings. At the same time, the women's discipleship group continued to grow. In response to the growth, Sameh added, "I chose potential leaders and focused my contribution on theological teaching and training in social ministry skills."

The ministry with the Bedouin is transforming the community around them. One person shared how she witnessed the change over time. "A woman used to come from the village and usually arrived in the middle of the Bible study meeting. She used to argue against what I was teaching. It caused a disturbance for all participants. However, she was touched with the life of the Messiah. Over time, her attitude and behaviour changed, to the extent that she brought her Ethiopian Christian domestic worker, saying she wanted her to learn about Jesus."

Sameh shared a similar story about a man named Abu Nizar.

> Abu is a Syrian refugee who lost his mother and his brother in
> an explosion and, when he went to get their bodies, his father
> passed away on the road from grief. Abu is a good reader in
> Islam and Christianity. He used to come and interrupt me during
> meetings when I taught about the goodness of God and his love for
> humanity. Abu used to say, "I do not believe in his goodness, I do
> not believe in his presence." After one year of attending meetings
> with us, he was touched with the love of the group. He felt the love
> of Jesus through his body, the church. He has become one of the
> leaders who help me conduct Bible study meetings.

Serving from the Margins: al-Minya, Upper Egypt

Many women in the Middle East are on the margins of society. Suzan is a
Christian leader in Upper Egypt who serves on the margins, working to see
the marginalized brought into the kingdom of God. She serves in al-Minya and
surrounding villages.[3] She leads a team of more than a hundred volunteers
who plant churches in villages.

Suzan grew up in a nominal Catholic Christian home. When she was in
high school, she felt in her heart that she wanted to work in a ministry that
serves the blind. For years in her ministry, she had a means of getting into
different homes and knowing multiple families. After a while she started to
work with a non-denominational organization owned by a Catholic priest.
Together they started to feel the need of teaching the Christian community
the Word of God. "We knew whole Christian villages that had no church
buildings and there was no Christian teaching, so we decided to cooperate with
leaders from different denominations to start planting home-based churches
in these places." Suzan started with the university graduates and the educated
housewives she knew in the five villages. She enthused them with the idea
of church planting and invited leaders from Cairo to train them. "The seed
started to sprout quickly, and the passion spread from one village to another."

The majority of leaders who serve here are women. They have risen from
the margins to teach the Word of God to other women, and from them the
whole household learns about Jesus. In Upper Egyptian communities, it is not

---

3. Al-Minya is a city of approximately 2 million people located 225 km (140 miles) south
of Cairo; it is the provincial centre of al-Minya governorate.

easy for women to move from house to house. It is a great challenge for women to serve in this atmosphere and that requires many sacrifices.

Suzan shared how she was about to get kidnapped one day when she was taking public transport from one village to another. "I was in a minibus when all the other passengers disembarked at one stop. The driver took another road in the desert, and I started to yell at him to stop the vehicle. God gave me the courage to jump from the bus when he was slowing down to take a turn. I ran until I found a car to pick me up. For me, the price of ministry includes risking security and life."[4]

The ministry in these remote poor areas has difficulties of various types.

> We have so many challenges; we suffer from the lack of deep theological teaching. In addition, we suffer from a lack of men participating in ministry since, typically, they prefer working instead of giving time for ministry. However, our greatest challenge comes from the church itself. Church leaders fear the consequences of our teaching and sometimes they think we want to convert people from one denomination to another. On occasions, they think we have a hidden agenda. Consequently, the church in some villages has prevented us from planting any home groups in their area.

Suzan and her team feel a great joy when they gather all the leaders from the different villages every three months to share their experiences and report how God is miraculously touching people's hearts. "So many people have been released from bad habits, so many families have found Christ's salvation, and so many sick people have been healed in the power of Jesus's name. The power of the house churches is like the power of the mustard seed; it is the kingdom of God, and we are honoured to be part of it."

A Community within the Community: Lebanese Druze

Chaden is a Druze woman.

> My husband, Riad, is a successful doctor. The Lebanese Civil War (see appendix) prompted us to move to Europe and build a new life. Many things happened to us in Romania. After the events of

---

4. Kidnapping of Christian women in Egypt is a complex topic, with accurate reporting limited by numerous cultural and legal factors. See for example, World Watch Monitor, *Egypt's disappearing Coptic women and girls*, 1 May 2018; accessed 19 December 2018; www.worldwatchmonitor.org/2018/05/egypts-disappearing-coptic-women-and-girls/.

11 September 2001 (9–11, see appendix) people changed their attitude towards us because we were regarded as Arab Muslims. Meanwhile, God was working in my husband's life to show him the right way. I had been very dedicated to Islam for two years at an earlier point in my life. Yet, my devotion was proving unsatisfactory to me. I cried, "Where are you God?" The one who responded was Jesus. We both came to faith, and we were hungry for knowing God. We were baptized in Romania and God showed us that he wanted us to return to Lebanon.

The Druze context is unique. It is a closed community with its own traditions and rules which are distinct within the Lebanese context. It is a religious and social society governed by inherited traditions, which puts firm boundaries between them and others. "Druze community is very specific, closed and full of mysterious tradition. In such a community, being Druze binds the individuals to their community, creating bonds that are frequently much stronger than nationality."

When the couple moved back to their Druze community, those around them noticed the changes in their attitudes and priorities. Chaden remarked that,

this is our society, and we have to serve them. Our belonging to this tribal society is very important for my husband's work as a doctor. Our society did not understand the nature of our faith, but God gave us the wisdom to identify ourselves as Druze who follow Jesus Christ. We have Jesus's teachings within our Druze beliefs, but they do not consider him to be divine. We used the ignorance of others about our Christian faith to respond to their questions and in doing so, we expressed our faith in Jesus to them.

For ten years, people from their community struggled to accept them. "Some family members and friends threatened to take our children away because we were not a good model." In their cultural values, the person who goes to God is a weak person; if they need something, then they seek God. "One day the Council of Elders met with Riad and his family, using their authority to threaten him that he would be rejected from the community if he continued to follow Jesus. Riad chose to remain true to his faith, and God blessed him richly in his work in spite of their intimidation."

The couple maintained their presence in the community. They were thinking of the best way they could serve their people and how they might be a blessing to them. "Church planting in our community has to come from within. We started a Bible study for five people at home. It started to grow as people who lived in different areas in the mountains called us and asked to participate because they were believers who needed to belong to the body of Christ. Within a few years it had reached one hundred participants."

This development prompted them to leave the church that they had been members of for ten years. They adapted the Bible study to be a church service appropriate to their Druze context. Chaden began formal study of theology, which enriched the biblical and missional understanding of what had become church. Their church grew rapidly, and some church members started similar groups in other Druze communities.

Their main challenge is how to transform their community to see God as Father, Son, and Holy Spirit, and how to help them receive salvation by grace when traditional Druze belief is salvation by deeds.

Missiological Reflection: From "A Church of a Dead Person" to "A Church of Raised Dead" (by Mary)

This reflection is based on the story of a church in a city in the Middle East. The author, the wife of the pastor, has requested anonymity in order to describe this church's experiences in church planting. It speaks of growth, decline and restoration, and it illustrates several elements of church planting. All names have been changed.

In 2007, my husband was appointed pastor of a church in a major city in the Middle East. The church was founded, planted, in the late 1960s in a rented house, under the leadership of Rev Marwan. It achieved official, legal recognition in 1970 under the auspices of a council representing churches of several protestant denominations. By 1992, the church had established additional churches with their own buildings in several towns in the same country. The funding for these church buildings came from foreign donors.

This period of growth and church planting did not endure. There was a marked change when Marwan was murdered in 1982. This was followed by rumours concerning who was responsible and disputes within the denomination's council which caused a crisis of confidence amongst its pastors. From 1986 to 2007 the church had very few attendees on Sundays, sometimes just four. Several of the other churches closed, with their buildings taken over for other purposes.

Of note during these difficult times is that Marwan's niece, Alia, focused on children's ministries. She made a positive contribution to the church, even if most of those she taught became active members of other churches.

In 2007, direct cooperation began between the church and my husband, Rev Timothy, who was given the title of Senior Pastor of the church where he ministered voluntarily, without a salary from the church. Instead, he and I continued to receive our income through the organization of which we are long-standing members. He brought the idea of adopting a spiritual multiplication model within this church, and he hoped that this model would become widespread throughout the country.

When we arrived, we noticed that what was important to the elders was for a pastor to preach on Sundays. The three elders were Marwan's brother, Paul, Paul's wife and Alia. At that time, they did not want, as a church, to be challenged spiritually nor to confront their fear of the government's secret police and the neighbouring churches who used to write negative reports against this church. I remember the first initiative that I led was putting a sign on the outer wall to the effect that this is a church building, a place of worship, and not an ordinary flat. It was like a miracle happened because it broke the fear that had lasted twenty-five years since the assassination. Maybe someone would deface or desecrate the building, or maybe more people would start attending, thereby increasing our pastoral responsibilities. The elders feared that they were not ready for this responsibility. We were all surprised by the blessing of the Lord on this church by breaking the wall of fear, and we willingly accepted the challenge of welcoming new members and training new, additional leaders.

In 2010, the church baptized six new members, an occasion that was seen as a revival. By the end of 2010, the regular attendance had risen to one hundred-twenty. In 2011, a new strategy for the church was developed. One element was that the youth meeting formed their own leadership committee. In 2012, the work of all committees was formally structured, and during 2013, new leaders were added to the church's ministries. The church baptized twenty-three new members that year.

This church, like all others, exists in a context. The political and civil environment started to change with the eruption of the Arab Spring (see glossary). There were significant developments taking place around the church's location during the following years. People were affected in many ways: some experienced civil disturbance, some suffered significant loss, and there was migration to and from the neighbourhood. The migration involved Muslims, Christians and others, including some with Church leadership responsibilities. Timothy and I saw these developments as an opportunity. Our church provided spiritual, psychological and material assistance to many. The number of people attending the church increased, reaching a thousand adult members plus four hundred-seventy children during 2016. This necessitated an expansion of the church building.

For many years, the church had wanted to expand its building, but chose not to attempt to do so: fears of how the governmental system might react, together with potential complaints from neighbours, formed an apparently inescapable barrier. But miracles do not depend on funding. Timothy seized an opportunity that arose when the church building was damaged during a disturbance. Timothy oversaw an enlargement as part of the repair. He encouraged the labourers and the elders who felt constrained and spiritually frozen by their local context.

At the conclusion of the work, pastors from many churches, who had been squabbling for decades, gathered together. Among them was the head of a council of Protestant churches who was able to observe this church's growth in numbers and transformation of its building, and subsequently used it as a model for other churches in the region.

It was a privilege to see a thousand people attending a place of worship that had four people in 2007. The journey from a situation of no hope of expansion began with a pastor who loved, respected and dreamt with the existing leaders.

This historical review prompts consideration of one aspect of church planting, namely leadership style.

The leadership structure of the church changed to become community-based. It encouraged faithful believers to serve the church. The senior pastor leads the church by preaching the Bible, caring for believers, spreading the gospel to the non-believers, praying for the sick and taking care of the poor as well as strengthening the fellowship among believers through the Lord's Supper and Baptism. He also works with many other pastors to build churches in the different communities they serve, causing a spiritual movement across the country.

In leadership style, the national and regional context is significant and influences the leadership of churches. In many places, political leadership is focused on one person or one family. This creates an expectation in many that pastoral leadership will conform to the same pattern: the pastor can be the soul of the church, acting as the one leader who rules for years and whose influence endures after his death. This aspect can put a lot of responsibility on the next generation of pastors: will they retain "the one man" style or will they teach and model different broader, more inclusive leadership styles? They may revive or poison churches. Many people may well follow the so called "strong leader." Is this healthy, even biblical?

The establishment of the church can also be considered within the scope of the "internal" mission. The founding sponsor was one of the fruits of the missionary training, who returned after his studies to serve in his country in the same way that the assassinated pastor who planted the church went to his hometown to establish additional new churches. He brought support from the West for the construction of new church buildings and for regional expansion. Unfortunately, these churches are closed today because of the appointment of a volunteer who was eighty-six years old. He closed the churches and used the buildings to rent out to different people for personal financial benefit. In the realm of external mission only, the enthusiasm of some Western missionaries was to teach English in schools, thinking that they could expose people to the Word of God by showing them the English translation of the Bible.

Al-marhoum is an Arabic word that talks about the dead person whose sins have been forgiven. As a cultural gratitude to the murdered pastor, the church elders retained the idea of respecting what they thought he would do in each situation. Yet over time, and being small in number, their dreams became frustrated. When the church grew, the four elders continued thinking how the dead pastor would act. In some sense, they were raising him up from death, for example in his attitudes. This is culturally deeply respectful of the leader whose memory remains in the heart of those who knew him.

Editorial Reflection: What Is a Church? Who Builds the Church?

So, what is a church? And who builds the church? Jesus Christ has one church which has numerous local expressions, many of which are members of a denomination.

In this chapter we have described local churches that meet discreetly in homes and those that are recognized legal entities and operate church buildings. One exception is the emergence of online churches, groups of Christians who meet regularly using online tools. The potential for this has existed for at least a decade; the known existence of such churches in the MENA region is a more recent development. Such groups always operate discreetly, avoiding publicity and requiring a personal invitation and introduction to anyone wishing to join them.

So, what is a church? Immediately we must discount that a church is defined by a building. However, it is worth noting that buildings are of profound significance to many Christians throughout the Middle East. Having a building marked with symbols of the faith is a sign of belonging, of being part of society. Further, within Eastern Orthodox and Oriental Orthodox churches, the architecture of the building is significant. For example, the view that the grace of God is mediated by touch means that the presence of an iconostasis (see glossary) plays a central role in worship. One consequence is that denial of a church building with certain architectural features amounts to denial of worship in its fullest form. For these churches, the establishment, or planting, of new churches requires the construction of a church building with specific features.

So how should we define a church? We will start with considering what church worship or a church service comprises. One list of required elements would be some form of worship, the reading of Scripture, prayer and a sense of community including mutual care and support. The exact form of many of these elements varies widely. For example, worship usually comprises music and singing although poetry is an alternative in some cultures.

We could then define a church as a group of people who meet for a service regularly, typically weekly or as their context allows.

We need to add two further elements that are practised consistently, but not necessarily weekly. These are the use of sacraments and a sense of discipline. The latter is keeping members accountable to God and biblical ethics. In many Western contexts, this operates in subtle, discreet ways. Many small group-based evangelism and discipleship programmes have obedience to Scripture embedded within their methodology.

Sacrament varies amongst denominations, typically including Baptism and re-enactment of the Last Supper, referred to as Communion, Eucharist, Mass and Lord's Supper by various church denominations.

For Catholic Christians, the highest form of worship is the Mass, since it is in this rite that the worshipper meets most fully with Jesus. Conducting Mass requires a duly authorized priest. One consequence is that for members of Catholic churches, the lack of available priests amounts to a denial of worship. Further, the planting of a new church requires the availability of a priest. This makes the training of priests a critical component of church planting, something that we will return to in chapter 10.

A further reflection on music is that as a community of Christ-followers emerges within a socio-ethnic group, they initially rely on songs imported from other groups, either Middle Eastern or beyond. As the group grows numerically, they begin to write their own worship songs to express biblical truth using their own cultural and linguistic background.

In conclusion, Dietrich Bonhoeffer reminds us what is rightly our part and what is God's part in church planting:

But it is not we who build. No man builds the church but Christ alone. Whoever is minded to build the church is surely well on the way to destroying it; for he will build a temple to idols without wishing or knowing it. We must confess, he builds. We must proclaim, he builds. We must pray, he builds. . . . It is a great comfort which Christ gives to his church: you confess, preach, bear witness to me and I alone will build where it pleases me. Do not meddle in what is my province.[5]

This is particularly pertinent as new churches are planted, especially those for whom most members are from non-Christian backgrounds. Local context is crucial to what forms new churches will take.

---

5. Dietrich Bonhoeffer, *No Rusty Swords: Letters, Lectures and Notes from the Collected Works of Dietrich Bonhoeffer*, eds. Edwin H. Robertson and John Bowden (London: Collins, 1970), 212.

3

Discipleship in the Mission of God

We continue our journey from evangelism through the establishment of fellowships and churches to the development of Christian understanding within each follower of Christ.

Our considerations are provided by Ivan Fawzi, assisted by Chris Todd and Samah Fakhreldein (see contributors' bios).

Background: Inside Church Buildings and Homes (by Chris Todd)

Contemporary discipleship in Lebanon is a spectrum of approaches, some of which have been brought here after being successful in other regions, and others, which are more local in origin. The diversity of Lebanese culture and ethnicity means that no single approach to discipleship has emerged that is sufficient for every context.

Historically, the Roman Catholic church was a pioneer in evangelism and discipleship among the people of Lebanon. A major landmark in Catholic missions and discipleship was the founding in 1622 of the Congregation for the Propagation of the Faith by Pope Gregory XV. This established unified goals, rules of conduct and clarification of methods. Compulsion and threats were banned, and missionaries were encouraged to choose "sweet and loving ways" which included patience, setting a good example, good works and rational persuasion.[1]

Each mission was under the authority of a religious order and had priorities aligned with those of that order with an overall goal of uniting

---

1. Habib Badr, ed., "Catholic Missions in the Middle East," in *Christianity: A History in the Middle East* (Beirut: MECC, 2005), 692.

Eastern Christians with Rome.[2] The Capuchins (see glossary) brought small, mobile groups who spread quickly in the region with specific goals and a plan to establish an ecumenical movement. The Jesuits served the spiritual needs of Western communities, as well as forming societies and fraternities for preaching, teaching and the translation of religious texts into Arabic. Dominicans (see glossary) founded schools which taught in Arabic to serve Muslims and engaged in scholarly Islamic studies. All of these orders continued to expand their presence by the establishment of structured discipleship centres such as schools, monasteries, libraries, seminaries, theological colleges and universities in the region.[3]

Evangelical missionaries first came to the Levant (see glossary) with the aim of converting Jews to the Christian faith. Unable to settle in Jerusalem, they made their first headquarters in Beirut in 1823. They planted churches throughout the region and soon set about establishing schools, including the first schools for girls in the Middle East. They also worked on translating the Scriptures and imported the first printing press in the region to establish a Christian publishing house. They also established universities, including the American University of Beirut, which is arguably the most prestigious university in the region. Subsequent evangelical missionary efforts built upon this idea of discipleship through the establishment of educational institutions.[4]

Until more recent decades, discipleship had depended heavily upon such institutional structures. Innovations, like radio, television and satellite programming as well as Internet channels, were added into an already existing framework of formal education. (*We shall return to this in chapter 8.*) Gospel preaching, Bible and literature distribution, and church-based Sunday School instruction were all standard components of discipleship and remain so today. These are all approaches that would be familiar in any Western country and include personal discipleship and mentoring. Speaking for those today who continue with this approach, evangelist, disciple-maker, and missionary Georges Houssney says, "I give new disciples books to read, videos to watch, CDs to listen to and Internet sites to visit. Those are aids, but not substitutes for a relationship: literature and media cannot replace personal time with them."[5]

The 1980s were a time of great change with regard to discipleship, both worldwide and in Lebanon. Young Western Christians, emboldened by the

---

2. Badr, "Catholic Missions," 690.

3. Badr, 694–695.

4. Badr, 717–719.

5. Georges Houssney, *Engaging Islam* (Treeline Publishing, 2010) Kindle Locations 2015–2017.

Jesus movements of the 1970s, began answering the call to frontier missions among the world's least reached people groups (see glossary, people group). As David Garrison observed: "Near the top of every list were the world's one billion unreached Muslims."[6] A growing backdrop of voices (including Virginia Cobb, Michael Goldsmith, John Anderson and John Wilder) in the 1960s and 1970s had begun calling for a new understanding of how Muslims could follow Christ,[7] and how discipleship should be done in a Muslim context. An article by J. Dudley Woodberry in 1989 provided one of the first case studies of an "insider movement" consisting of Muslim disciples of Christ who retain a Muslim identity.[8]

These academic discussions of highly "contextualized" movements were based on the observation of events already happening on the ground among disciple makers. Pastor Fouad Accad, long-time Chairman of the Bible Society in Lebanon, had for decades been advocating and practising discipleship among Muslims within their own contexts. He described a shift in the overall practice of discipleship among workers in the Middle East: "Actually, the old-type missionary is gradually disappearing from most parts of the Arab world. In his place, a new type is emerging by the tens of thousands: guest workers migrating as teachers, engineers, foremen, artisans, doctors . . . labourers, etc."[9] These new workers often moved into Islamic communities and worked within the context of that community. Accad, a pioneer in contextualization, observed: "It would be insensitive – in fact, negligent – if we were to completely disregard the Qur'an. Why? Because it would be difficult, if not impossible, to discuss spiritual things with Muslims if we ignore their primary spiritual guidebook."[10]

Coinciding with this shift in approaches to discipleship, David Garrison documented the beginning of a great movement toward Christ in the Muslim world. There is a clear correlation between the two developments – a new generation of missionaries with new ideas of discipleship and the emergence

---

6. David Garrison, *A Wind in the House of Islam: How God Is Drawing Muslims around the World to Faith in Jesus Christ* (WIGTake Resources, LLC., 2014) Kindle Locations 298–299.

7. Harley Talman and John J. Travis, eds., "Historical Development of the Insider Paradigm," in *Understanding Insider Movements: Disciples of Jesus within Diverse Religious Communities* (Pasadena: William Carey Library, 2016), Kindle Locations 1029–1075.

8. J. Dudley Woodberry, "Contextualization among Muslims: Reusing Common Pillars," in *The Word among Us: Contextualizing Theology for Mission Today*, ed. Dean S. Gilliland (Dallas: Word Books, 1989), 282–312.

9. Fouad Accad, "The Qur'an: A Bridge to Christian Faith," *Missiology: An International Review* (July 1976), 332.

10. Fouad Accad, *Building Bridges: Christianity and Islam* (Colorado Springs: Navpress, 1997), 12.

of unprecedented movements to Christ among Muslims. David Garrison believes there is a causal relationship link. He writes, "one reason we are seeing movements to Christ today, that we were not seeing in centuries past, is we are conducting outreach to Muslims in ways that differ from ages past." He describes the new generation of workers as "gospel fishermen" who are "introducing colloquial Muslim-idiom translations of the Scripture, Muslim-focused outreach and ministry, contextualized witness, satellite television and radio broadcasts, prayer walking, Qur'anic bridging and other innovative approaches."[11]

The religious diversity of Lebanon – there are eighteen officially recognized religious sects – means that discipleship happens in a wide variety of contexts. Many Lebanese who are reluctant to seek out discipleship within traditional church and institutional settings for personal reasons are being discipled in home and community-based contexts. Discovery Bible Study (DBS) is one such programme that is finding increased use among disciple-makers in Lebanon. DBS encourages home and community-based groups within a disciple's own culture, an asset in a country like Lebanon with such a variety of ethnic and cultural groups.

DBS emphasizes discipleship as a process of developing obedience to the Scriptures as they are studied. A disciple-maker (or group leader) begins with a series of twenty-six Bible readings[12] which are presented to the disciple one at a time in a sequential order. These passages outline the story and nature of Jesus from the creation to the ascension. Rather than teaching the disciple an interpretation of the Scriptures, the disciple is encouraged to hear the Scripture, retell or rewrite it, and determine how it should be obeyed.[13] The disciple is then encouraged to share this observation with others in his or her life. In this way DBS is meant to be multiplicative: it links discipleship to evangelism and church planting.

One concern in Lebanon is that DBS (as well as other highly contextualized approaches to discipleship) encourages new believers to avoid the institutional church, and even to have no love for the church. However, as DBS proponent Joseph Cumming points out:

---

11. Garrison, *Wind in the House*, Kindle Locations 3459–3466.

12. David Watson and Paul Watson, *Contagious Disciple Making: Leading Others on a Journey of Discovery* (Nashville: Thomas Nelson, 2014), 235–237.

13. Watson and Watson, 155.

Scripture also calls fellowships to recognize the unity and universality of the worldwide body of Christ. Some (highly contextualized) fellowships, and some workers partnering with them, have very negative views of, or broken relationships with (non-Muslim background believer) churches. Other (highly contextualized) fellowships have healthy attitudes toward the wider church.[14]

So, a properly aligned DBS will encourage fellowship with the greater body of Christ, and this should be encouraged and emphasized as this approach is used increasingly in Lebanon and elsewhere.

Editorial Reflection: Disciple Making Movements

Reference to DBS prompts a reflection on a related approach that has become widely used in some countries since approximately 2014. This is Disciple Making Movements which seek the rapid multiplication of small groups of people meeting to explore the claims of Christ. This approach is often based on DBS although other series of passages for Bible studies can be used. It employs a similar small-group methodology intended to instil obedience to Scripture, prayer and regular Bible reading in those exploring Christ or in those who are at an early stage of following him. A more detailed analysis of this together with how to evaluate its applicability is available online.[15] DBS resources are available in many languages.

Another resource is al Massira (the journey), whose strap line is "An open place: To walk with the Prophets and meet the Messiah."[16] This was developed as an evangelism tool but is also used as a discipleship tool amongst new disciples of Jesus. It comprises thirteen films with discussion questions for small groups. It was produced in Arabic and subsequently subtitled and dubbed into other languages. It is an example of a missional resource developed for the Middle East that is being used more broadly.

---

14. Talman and Travis, "Historical Development," Kindle Locations 1274–1277.

15. Global Connections, *Disciple Making Movements (DMM)*, 17 February 2017, accessed 29 October 2018; www.globalconnections.org.uk/sites/newgc.localhost/files/papers/2017_dmm_-_towards_best_practices.pdf.

16. www.almassira.org/ (accessed 5 December 2018).

Case Studies (by Samah Fakhreldein)

> *Our three case studies take us to Egypt and Sudan before returning to Lebanon.*

Walk with Them, Experience their Life

Ehab is an Egyptian medical doctor who served in the army for several years. He came from a nominal Coptic Christian family, where faith came naturally because they were born into a Christian family. When he was a young doctor serving his early years in the army, he learned several lessons about minoritization (see glossary) and living in the margins. He felt that he was persecuted simply for being a Christian. For years, he kept the bitterness in his heart thinking that only Christians are persecuted in Egypt. In the 1990s, there was a wave in the Coptic Orthodox church in Egypt, in which some former priests promoted being born again and taught about the role of the Holy Spirit in the lives of people, the church and the world. At that time Ehab and his wife submitted their lives to Jesus and decided to live and practise their faith. Ehab started to study the Word of God, and he started to share these studies with a group of Christian villagers in a poor area where he worked. He initiated and ran what he knew later to be discipleship meetings. Ehab learned by practise how to study the Word of God, apply it to his life and share it with others.

Ehab and his family moved to Cairo, and he started to serve with a church where he found the need for leaders who make disciples. The nature of his discipleship programmes was different this time: his disciples were not from a Christian background. "At the beginning, I did not know where to start. Their background, culture and values were completely different. I had been struggling, just to feel with them and understand what they felt during their faith transformation process. In Egypt converting to Christianity is considered infidelity and is violently rejected by society." His ministry with this socially rejected group opened his mind to seeing the kingdom of God differently. He started to practise his love for his oppressors. He started to experience dangerous situations and felt God's hand in the face of possible death. "It was not easy to walk with them and experience their life. I remember how it was hard for us as a group when we lost a member because of the social persecution or when we heard that a brother or a sister was arrested and tortured by the authorities for their faith. I think this is the price of discipleship."

For Ehab, discipleship is a decision and life transformation process. "When we submit ourselves to Jesus, he gets our souls, but our mindsets might stay the same. Discipleship is the process when the Holy Spirit and our freewill work together to change our old nature and to be new in Christ." He uses the Bible as his foundation in the discipleship process, as he categorized the discipleship stages as the human growth stages and studied the Bible accordingly.

One of the stories Ehab shared concerned a man who came from a non-Christian background. This man was a religious leader in his village who promoted terrorism and violence towards Christians. When he accepted Jesus's salvation and became a disciple, he ceased to do this. Instead, he promoted righteousness and truth in the name of Christ. One problem was he used to beat his wife. He came to Ehab and said, "I am a Christian, I believe in Jesus, but I still beat my wife at home. What shall I do? I do not know how to change." For Ehab the challenge was how to help the man to live in a Jesus-like manner in all aspects of his life and relationships. It was not enough to know the truth and dare to share it: the important thing is to live the truth and to bear witness to it.

Building the Church in Disorienting Times

Barnaba is an educated Christian youth leader from Sudan. At times, he endured persecution from Sudanese Muslim neighbours. He lived through his country's division in 2011 when South Sudan seceded, a political development that affected the complex relationships amongst Sudan's ethnically diverse and religiously varied communities.[17]

Barnaba started a ministry called Focus among university students. The objective was to provide discipleship and spiritual support during the critical stage of development that happens at this age. His goal was to help the students to feel that they belonged to God's community and to live as members of God's family.

Barnaba was a seminary student. The tools he got from learning theology and how to apply what he learned in real life helped him to shape his understanding of real discipleship. "For us, discipleship is a lifetime process. We do discipleship through life groups, as we study the Word of God together. We learn, worship and pray together. When I was a university student, this was the main thing that I longed for. Therefore, I know how life groups are very supportive for the students."

Barnaba and his ministry in Focus concentrated on sharing kingdom ethics through their fellowship. "Integrity in leadership is one important value that

---

17. See, for example, Andrews, *Identity Crisis*, 136–140.

we try to maintain. We believe that we are role models for our disciples and we must act accordingly. Our values have to be reflected in our lives."

Barnaba's life changed dramatically. One day he was arrested by the authorities who confiscated his possessions and investigated his ministry. After a long interrogation, the authorities released him. However, he was unable to continue his ministry in Sudan. Barnaba fled to Egypt as a refugee.

In Egypt, he restarted his ministry with almost three thousand Sudanese refugee students from different religious backgrounds. "Our vision is to build future leaders from the youth, who reject the wars and corruption, who speak the truth, and who witness to Christ. Our objective is to help the youth live according to kingdom ethics."

Barnaba used his pain and homesickness to get the power for serving the Sudanese church in Egypt. The methodology he uses for discipleship is based on having fellowship with the students, sharing their challenges and needs as one family. "If we want to make disciples, we have to live the disciples' life. We live as brothers and sisters in one family. We live the love of Christ and support each other in these hard times."

Barnaba's dream is to see disciples who are empowered and leading others in new locations. He thinks that there is always a need for workers, more people able to disciple others. For him good workers, good disciple-makers, are crucial.

Discipleship as a Journey for Life and a Journey for Reconciliation

Lebanon has a long and wounded history including a civil war and occupations by its neighbours (see appendix). In the midst of the unhealed wounds, the Syrian crisis came up, and a large number of Syrians fled into Lebanon. The hardest part was when the Lebanese church started to respond to the crises and open its doors to these displaced persons.

Hikmat Kashouh is a Lebanese theologian and the pastor of the Resurrection Church.[18] He was born around the start of the Lebanese Civil War. He experienced all the woes of that war as a child and teenager. His family migrated from one place to another, and his wider family lost their house and relatives. Hikmat grew up in a Christian home, but his family did not have a personal relationship with God. At the age of seventeen, he experienced Jesus's salvation, and he started to have a personal relationship with God. He recalls

---

18. A fuller version of this case study is in Hikmat Kashouh, *Following Jesus in Turbulent Times* (Carlisle: Langham Global Library, 2018).

that, "one of my friends invited me to attend a spiritual meeting, and there I felt real peace in my heart for the first time. It was not an ordinary peace; it was God's peace which was beyond any imagination. I started to feel love towards God and towards people, and from that day my whole life has changed."

Hikmat leads a church of eleven different nationalities. A majority of the congregation are refugees from Iraq or Syria. More than half of church members are from non-Christian backgrounds. Many members are participants in one of many small groups referred to as "life groups." "A uniform church combines people with the same social level and the same beliefs, mindset and practice; but when the church assembles people with diverse ethnic backgrounds, that creates a ground for conflict. Therefore, in the last five years the church has learned how to live and coexist despite the different backgrounds of its members. We observe during our worship gatherings how God placed in this church all these people from different backgrounds and how he taught us to genuinely love one another despite our diversity."

The discipleship system which Hikmat had set up for the whole church, together with his insistence on including all the church members in the discipleship life groups, was the main reason behind their success in growing in faith as one church. In their discipleship programme, the church experiences being one family as they study the Word of God through the life groups and live according to it. They use the Discovery Bible Study methodology, which suits the diverse backgrounds and the different levels of education. Hikmat notes that, "this gave us spiritual maturity, and has enriched and prospered this church."

The vision of the church is to "love God, love your neighbour." Therefore, when the Syrian crisis started, the church started to apply what they believed and to respond by opening their doors to the Syrians. It was not an easy thing to do, as they, along with the whole of Lebanon, had suffered for years from the Syrian army's oppression in Lebanon. Every Lebanese family has a sad story they remember from that period: some lost relatives, others were injured, obliging them to live with disability. The Sunday school leader in the church described how a bullet hit her in her eye when she was a child. She lost that eye and lives with a disability. "It was very hard for me as a human being to love people whom I considered my enemies. Now I teach hundreds of their children, and I feel that I am so blessed to do this ministry in the kingdom of God."

Walking the disciple's road is not easy; there is always a cost. To have one church with diverse backgrounds is full of challenges. Hikmat notes, "We face so many social challenges, financial challenges, but the most important challenge is the unity of the family. We focus on both spiritual growth and fulfilment of practical needs. Our focus is on building healthy relationships as one church family. Our focus is to disciple disciples who make disciples."

Missiological Reflection: The Call of Discipleship in the Muslim World and Beyond (by Ivan Fawzi)

He called the crowd to him along with his disciples and said: "Whoever wants to be my disciple must deny themselves and take up their cross and follow me. For whoever wants to save their life will lose it, but whoever loses their life for me and for the gospel will save it" (Mark 8:34–35).

To say that we are living in extraordinary times is an understatement. We are witnessing how God the Father through Christ and by the Spirit is acting within the Muslim world. The sheer numbers of those who are engaging with, enquiring about, and learning from the Bible about the Christian faith is unprecedented. Many have fully embraced and accepted Jesus as Saviour and Lord – something that has not happened on the present scale since Islam entered into world history in the seventh century.

Why is this happening? Is this shift, as Chris Todd explained above, caused by the death of the "old type" of missions, replaced with new methodologies and contextual approaches? Might the hand and purposes of God be at work behind the scenes through regional and international uprisings and downfalls? Do political, religious or sociological powers have something to do with it? Certainly, we see significant breakthroughs when ideologies are unmasked as bankrupt, leading to disillusionment from within. Systems are toppled and regimes that we thought were unshakable end up crumbling. Perhaps this is what is happening within the house of Islam in our day. Since Ayatollah Al Khomeini took over in Iran in 1979 vast numbers of Persians came to faith in Christ. Similarly, the atrocities of the Algerian civil conflict of the 1990s were the backdrop to the emergence of a church amongst the Kabyle (see glossary) people. More recently, in the aftermath of the Arab Spring (see glossary and appendix), the rise of ISIS (see glossary) and the ensuing refugee crisis, we have seen the gospel advancing in the Muslim world. Or perhaps the seed blood of martyrs – those who lived as true disciples amongst Muslims by loving, serving and even dying for Jesus – is finally bearing fruit?

It is clear from our case studies that there has been a significant shift in the hearts and minds of Christians towards their Muslim neighbours. This change in attitude is long overdue and is at the heart of Jesus's call to discipleship. When God's people take Jesus's call literally – in its entirety, without diluting its simplicity and clarity, without softening the demands and expectations of his call, when they live it out counter-culturally in the midst of the "other"[19] despite danger, threat and persecution – breakthroughs and transformation happen. Ground-breaking revivals[20] in the history of the church seem to happen when we take the simple words of Jesus for what they are and live them out fully and practically within our churches, fellowships or groups. Crowning him as Lord in our lives is worth losing everything because we gain all (Matt 13:44–45).

Karl Barth notes "that the New Testament never uses the word 'discipleship' (*akolouthesis*) as a substantive but only the verb 'follow' (*akolouthein*) or 'follow after me' (*opiso mou erchesthai*). Which means, to go after or behind someone . . . we must always remember that we are dealing with what is obviously in the New Testament view an event that cannot be enclosed in general concept."[21]

Christians often treat discipleship as a system or set of approaches, with a wide range of interpretations regarding application and implementation. Discipleship is, in essence, simply following Jesus. It means forsaking all, despite difficulties, suffering and even death, primarily death to self. Discipleship is in danger of getting lost in trendy terminologies and packaged programmes. Dietrich Bonhoeffer said:

> Revival of church life always brings in its train a richer understanding of Scriptures. Behind all the slogans and catchwords of ecclesiastical *(church)* controversy, necessary though they are, there arises a more determined quest for him who is the sole object of it all, for Jesus Christ himself . . . What we want to know is not what would this or that man, or this or that church have for us. But what Jesus Christ himself wants from us. When we go to church and listen to the sermon *(or meet in a group and read the Bible)* what we want to hear is his Word.[22]

Today, measuring whether or not discipleship is successful – never mind if it is actually true discipleship – seems to be based on numbers and whether a particular approach or methodology has been used. I am overwhelmed by the variety of "disciplenships" on offer and get lost in the supermarket of choices,

---

19. I am using the term "other" to describe anyone who is considered an outsider, whether religiously, socially, or morally. This includes church culture and, in our discussion, specifically relates to Muslims.

20. Perhaps this is the old-fashioned equivalent to "movements" and "multiplication." I am using it to refer to the mass turning of people towards Jesus Christ.

21. Karl Barth, *The Call to Discipleship* (Minnesota: Fortress Press, 2003 edition), 6, 3. Italics added, comma added.

22. Dietrich Bonhoeffer, *The Cost of Discipleship* (Danvers: SCM Press, 1959), 29.

which seem to focus on "hatching" new followers quickly. Now, when depth and maturity are most crucial, we still seem to be focused on numbers of followers, groups and leaders. The quality and maturity of disciples, both lay people and pastors/leaders, remains a challenge in Muslim ministry today. Undeniably there is some progress in this area, but there are few mature and established believers from Muslim backgrounds leading in their own community let alone Christian-background churches regionally and internationally. Given the high number of followers, we are clearly heading into danger if this imbalance is not addressed. For the "children of Ishmael" to take the place that God has called them to and to prepare them and us for the future, we need to bring back the simple and original meaning of discipleship: the act of following Jesus himself.

In a culture of "titles," "labels," "hierarchy" and "status" we need to be extra careful not to rob discipleship of its essence, meaning and purpose. An indiscriminate use of titles, such as "leader" or "pastor" can become a stumbling block to transformation into true Christlikeness. Bonhoeffer warns against what he calls "cheap grace," emptying the word of the true meaning of discipleship. It is costly and priceless not only because it cost God his Son but also it costs the disciple of Christ his or her own life:

> The Disciple is called to leave his old life behind and completely surrender. . . . Discipleship means adherence to Christ. An abstract Christology, a doctrinal system of a general religious knowledge on the subject of grace or on the forgiveness of sins, renders discipleship superfluous . . . With an abstract idea it is possible to enter into a relation of formal knowledge, to become enthusiastic about it, and perhaps even to put it into practice; but it can never be followed in personal obedience. Christianity without the living Christ is inevitably Christianity without discipleship, and Christianity without discipleship is always Christianity without Christ. It remains an abstract idea, a myth which has a place for the Fatherhood of God, but omits Christ as the living Son . . . in such a religion there is trust in God, but no following of Christ.[23]

Meetings, discussions and DBS are wonderful and must continue to be part of what we do, but we sometimes miss the centrality of Jesus in discipleship. General ideas about faith and ethical and moral behaviour can easily detract from the essence of discipleship. Some disciple-makers promote deductive studies with no or very little cross-referencing between Bible passages to ensure the main objective of quick and simple multiplication. I can understand and

---

23. Bonhoeffer, 49–50.

accept this if the focus and emphasis in the studies always point to the person and work of Christ – as eternal Word of God, mediator, rescuer, messenger, the one the law and prophets point to, etc. – and the triune God. However, rarely is this included or taught in the methodologies used for reaching out to Muslims. Therefore, discouraging any interpretation or instruction leads to a poor or even non-existent understanding of the Trinitarian nature of God and the Christ-centred revelation, particularly in Old Testament studies. It is as if we believe the Trinitarian nature of God belongs to an advanced academic doctrine, suitable for a later stage of discipleship and not so essential at the beginning.

No one, whether Muslim, Christian or any other background, approaches faith and Scripture objectively or impartially. We do not operate in a vacuum. Ehab, from our case studies, said that Jesus "gets our souls, but our mindsets might stay the same." Muslims could easily fit their understanding of the Christ that is presented in the Bible into a system or structure where they obey him yet continue to deny him as the crucified and risen Lord God.

A foundation is built for faithful discipleship when the centrality of Christ and the reality of the relational triune God is taught, understood, applied and lived out in day-to-day life. This is not a discussion about biblical principles, interpretations or doctrines, but it is an urgent reality we all face. Many Muslim enquirers stop following Christ and eventually fizzle out of churches, groups and fellowships due to disillusionment, severe pressures, circumstances or overt persecution. When is Trinitarian-focused discipleship supposed to happen? When and in what context will these communities of followers be exposed to what should be essential in the journey of discipleship? Bonhoeffer's words are crucial for us in our context today: God is blessing, multiplying and enriching the body of Christ – the church – with numerous new followers from Islam, often in remarkable and unexpected ways. The sleeping church is waking to God's heart for Muslims. The need for authentic discipleship is urgent. Helpful as they are, we do not need more resources, methods or training. We need to live out the revolutionary call of discipleship among Muslims.

Are we in tune with what the Father is doing in the world today, especially among Muslims? Does it worry you or fill you with excitement? Do you react to the growth and influence of Muslims with anxiety, fear and resentment? In 2017 various news reports stated that the most popular name given to new-born boys in London was Mohammad![24] Would this bring you joy or make you angry? Does it fill you with excitement and enthusiasm or something else?

---

24. The actual statistics vary, not least because of the numerous different spellings of Mohammad – one source lists fourteen. See for example any of the following which cover a variety of time frames but convey a similar message: www.bbc.com/news/uk-england-45638806

God is at work in the heart of the Middle East. Lebanon is a country where "difference" is not only seen but felt, lived and promoted. Many deep and bitter cultural, social, economic, political and religious divisions are found amongst the Lebanese themselves. Further divisions emerged with the arrival of many displaced Syrians and their impact on the economy and the Lebanese lifestyle. Add to this the bloody and pain-filled history between the Lebanese and Syrians, and the animosity seems irreconcilable in human terms.

Can any discipleship course, method, programme or approach make "Sharbel" the Lebanese Christian open his door and heart to the Syrian Muslim "Mohammad"? Story after story emerges today of those who, compelled by Christ's love alone, were reconciled to their "enemies." As true disciples they now serve Syrians wholeheartedly and as a result thousands of Muslims are trusting in Christ today.

God is at work when followers of Jesus reach out and step into the life of the "other." He moves when we start relating, mixing, talking and eating together in their homes as well as ours. These relationships expose our ignorance and display our vulnerabilities. We experience their life with its joys and hardships. We step into the unknown, the uncomfortable, the different; we cross into the camp of the "other," and through it all we learn discipleship because it is putting our money where our mouth is by walking in the footsteps of our Saviour. When the "other" stops being the "alien" and when it is no longer "us" and "them," then true discipleship happens. Our case studies demonstrate that discipleship is living and sharing the journey with all its pain and risk with full commitment to Jesus and his love. It is a reflection of the Trinity: it is relational.

God's amazing work in Lebanon offers numerous lessons for the worldwide church's understanding of discipleship, especially as more and more Muslims follow Jesus. Because Lebanon has certain freedoms that no other Muslim-majority country has, Muslims are seen publicly within the walls of traditional, institutional churches. They are reading the Bible and following Christ openly. Hundreds attend church while retaining their Islamic-cultural expressions. Many of us are learning through experience what a diverse, multicultural church needs to be, where both churched and unchurched believers – including Muslim background believers – are equal and one in Christ. This exposure is long overdue, essential and desperately needed. It is vital for the growth of the

---

(September 2018), www.dailymail.co.uk/news/article-4469826/Muhammed-Amelia-popular-baby-names-London.html (May 2017), www.independent.co.uk/news/uk/home-news/muhammad-boys-names-uk-list-william-replaced-a7958221.html (September 2017) (all accessed 12 December 2018).

church as we transcend the powerful divisions of nationality, ethnicity, sect and previous religious affiliations and live together as one in Christ.

What is your vision for the future of the church in the Arab world? The Muslim world? The rest of the world? What will we look like? God is preparing people from Muslim backgrounds today who will not be in the background but will be in the driver's seat of church. They are the future leaders, teachers, pastors, theologians, missionaries and missiologists. The church will be enriched by their contribution. We have a responsibility and calling to stand shoulder-to-shoulder, together as one, to worship, serve, witness, triumph, suffer and perhaps even die for each other. Yes, the challenges of discipleship among Muslims remain vast and there are no easy solutions. There will be no shortcuts in developing disciples of substantial depth, maturity and number. This is a call for all of us, no matter our background or location. The Father, Son and Holy Spirit are bringing more children into their fellowship. Look around you. The Muslim next door could become a brother or a sister. Are you willing to walk hand in hand with them and follow our beloved Master together?

4

Relief and Development in the Mission of God

We move our focus from spreading and teaching the Christian faith to look at some of the ways in which Jesus's followers live out their faith in daily life. What difference is Christianity making in the lives of its adherents, and how are those people affecting, influencing, changing and transforming the societies of which they are a part?

We are guided throughout by Rupen Das (see contributors' bios).

Background: The Face of Poverty (by Rupen Das)

The French writer and photographer Maxime du Camp arrived in Beirut in 1850 from Alexandria and wrote:

> Beirut is incomparable; not the city itself, which is pitiful and lacking in grandeur, but the country that surrounds it, the forest of parasol pines, the road bordered with nopals, myrtle, and pomegranate trees in which chameleons run; the view of the Mediterranean and the aspect of the wooded summits of the Lebanon that draw the purity of their lines on the sky. It is a retreat for the contemplative, for the disillusioned, for those who have been wounded by existence; it seems to me that one can live happily there doing nothing but looking at the mountains and the sea.[1]

About the same time Henri Guys, the former French consul, wrote that Beirut now had "consulates from almost every nation, commercial

---

1. Quoted in Samir Kassir, *Beirut* (London: University of California Press, 2010), 109.

establishments, hotels, well stocked stores, a European pharmacy, and finally a casino – a luxury that only ports of the first rank can permit themselves."[2]

It would seem that time has stood still over the past one hundred-sixty years. While the architecture has changed from three-storied sandstone coloured buildings with red tiled roofs to modern high-rise blocks, the essence of the city as a vibrant commercial and educational centre has remained. With so few immediately visible physical scars left from the civil war or even from the 2006 war (see appendix), the impression of Lebanon is that it is regaining its reputation as the tourist and resort destination in the Middle East.

In spite of all the physical reconstruction, there are dark threads and shadows that weave through the fabric of Lebanese society that are often not visible. The 2008 United Nations Development Programme (UNDP) Country Study on Lebanon stated that 20.59 percent of the Lebanese population (excluding refugees) were poor and an additional 7.97 percent were extremely poor.[3] More than a quarter of the population lived below the poverty line, with the extremely poor "clustered far below the upper poverty line."[4] These statistics have deteriorated since the beginning of the Syrian crisis in 2011 and the huge influx of refugees into Lebanon, which has strained the social and economic fabric of the country.[5]

It is widely accepted that Lebanon has a population of about 4.1 million, though no accurate statistics exist as there has been no census since 1931. About 87 percent of the population lives in urban areas with about 1.8 million in the greater Beirut area.[6] Lebanon is politically, religiously and ethnically very complex, with many different communities and confessions vying for control socially, economically and politically. The country is composed of eighteen recognized religious communities.[7] In 2016 Lebanon was also home to at least 1.2 million displaced Syrians, more than 275,000 Palestinian refugees and

---

2. Quoted in Kassir, 109.

3. Extreme poverty in Lebanon is defined as "unable to meet their most basic food and non-food needs" in H. Laithy, K. Abu-Ismail and K. Hamdan, *Country Study: Poverty, Growth and Income Distribution in Lebanon* (Brasilia: International Poverty Center, UNDP, 2008), 4, 46.

4. Laithy, Abu-Ismail and Hamdan, 6.

5. More recent statistics are not available; one factor is the political situation which limits the effectiveness of central government.

6. United Nations Human Settlement Programme (UN-HABITAT), *Country Programme Document 2008–2009: Lebanon* (Nairobi: United Nations Human Settlement Programme, 2008), 6.

7. Alawite, Armenian Catholic, Armenian Orthodox, Assyrian Church of the East, Chaldean Catholic, Coptic, Druze, Greek Catholic, Greek Orthodox, Isma'ili, Jewish, Maronite, Protestant, Roman Catholic, Sunni, Shi'a, Syriac Catholic, Syriac Orthodox.

large numbers of foreign workers from countries such as Egypt, Bangladesh, Sri Lanka, the Philippines and Ethiopia.

One of the legacies of the Lebanese Civil War has been the emergence of new groups of vulnerable people. Examples include the Bedouins, the Dom people (see glossary), migrant workers and more specifically foreign domestic workers, refugees and children, notably street children and those born to refugees, prisoners or migrant workers. Child labour is a reality not only in the urban areas but also in many of the rural areas. This is in addition to the traditionally rural poor who live in pockets in the north, in the Bekaa Valley and in the south.[8]

The traditionally poor also includes Lebanese who have migrated from the rural areas to the urban centres. Because of the lack of opportunities and the high cost of housing, they live in urban slums or slum-like conditions. Not only is 28.54 percent of the population below the national poverty line, but the new vulnerable groups, many of whom do not have Lebanese citizenship, number more than a million and a half people, another 30 percent of the population. While all may not be poor, most are vulnerable and live on the edges of poverty with very few resources to withstand any emergencies or shocks.

Poverty is manifested in a variety of ways. Those who do not have citizenship cannot access healthcare or education. Most of the poor work in the informal sector and as a result do not have consistent work and are often without any income during the winter months when the weather is inclement, or when there is war or violence. They also have low levels of education and very few vocational skills, with little or no access to gain any kind of skills training. Because they did not have formal jobs they were not entitled to the national insurance schemes.

Other factors that have contributed to poverty across the country are the lack of any kind of social safety net. Further, unlike many Lebanese, they lack foreign remittances coming from family and relatives abroad. These vulnerabilities combine to create a downward spiral that not only increases their vulnerability but also ensures that communities remain poor from one generation to the next.

What makes the face of poverty different in a country like Lebanon is that poverty cannot be addressed only by ensuring access to services and subsidies, or by improving livelihoods and income. These are valuable interventions and will prevent extreme poverty but will rarely improve the socio-economic status

---

8. For a detailed study of poverty in Lebanon see Rupen Das and Julie Davidson, *Profiles of Poverty: The Human Face of Poverty in Lebanon* (Beirut: Dar Man al Hayat, 2011).

of the poor and enable them to move out of poverty. The confessional and communal structure of Lebanese society does not allow for social mobility. So, while the poor may be able to access education up to a basic level, they are unable to move out of chronic poverty and remain vulnerable.

Case Study – a Local Church in Eastern Lebanon (by Rupen Das)

This case study describes a church in the Bekaa Valley of Lebanon, just a few kilometres from the Syrian border. This church started as a home group and grew into a congregation of sixty adults. In presenting this, I am drawing on material from an unpublished PhD thesis by Elie Haddad, the President of the ABTS, and from my own experience of partnering with this church from the beginning of the Syrian refugee crisis in Lebanon.

As Syrian refugees began to flood into Lebanon in 2011, many of the over 1.2 million Syrian refugees settled in informal settlements or in any kind of shelter available in the Bekaa Valley. The refugees proved to be a challenge, not just because of the large numbers that came, but also because of the prior Syrian occupation of Lebanon, commonly dated as 1976 to 2005 (see appendix). Most Lebanese families have stories of having experienced atrocities committed by the Syrian military during the occupation.

The beginning of the church's work among Syrian refugees started with God working in the heart of the pastor as he was convicted to forgive the Syrians for what they had done to his family. His example encouraged others in the church to move beyond their negative feelings towards Syrian refugees. With assistance from the Lebanese Society for Educational and Social Development (LSESD – also known as the Lebanese Baptist Society), they started providing food-aid packages to a hundred refugee families. This grew to the extent that they were providing assistance to over a thousand families. They established a school for three hundred refugee children, informal schools in two other locations for another two hundred-fifty children and income generation projects for refugees. Partnerships with other agencies and groups provided medical services to those who would otherwise not be able to access medical care.

The church is very aware that it is not a social service agency but a church; helping refugees is considered part of its witness to Christ and his kingdom. They are very clear about their identity as a Christian evangelical church. Their help does not come with conditions, and recipients are not required to take any spiritual books or attend any meetings or church services; assistance is provided on the basis of need, regardless of religion or ethnicity. However, Christian materials are available, and they are invited to church services and meetings. As a result, many have attended and taken Christian materials. Further, the church runs DBS groups in many informal settlements.

The traditional teaching in Lebanese Baptist churches was that the church focuses exclusively on spiritual issues; social and humanitarian work is the responsibility of humanitarian agencies. However, the pastor of this church had a broader understanding of what ministry entailed. The majority of its members had come to faith and grown spiritually at the church in Zahle. There were not many transfer members. As a result, they grew up with the teaching that ministry involved meeting both the spiritual and physical needs of people.

The church was not prepared for this type of ministry. The growth of the ministry took them by surprise. They did not have the required people, the expertise, the experience, or the facilities. The church responded by empowering people to make decisions and by giving them specific responsibilities. The ministry flourished because of this delegation of responsibilities. Many leaders have since emerged, including many Syrian refugees who have come to faith and have become members of the church.

There was a lot of resistance from neighbours because of the traffic congestion and crowds during the food distributions. It being a Christian neighbourhood, many were also uncomfortable with Muslim men and women congregating there, with their different ways of dressing. They were also concerned about potential security threats. They protested regularly and filed complaints with the municipality, accusing the church of exacerbating religious tensions.

The church responded positively to the concerns of their Lebanese neighbours. They organized their food distributions and other activities so that it would not cause problems for those living around the church. They started helping the Lebanese poor as well in order to defuse the resentment that only the Syrians were receiving assistance. Over time, the neighbours began to appreciate the work of compassion that the church was doing.

There was no conditionality in the assistance that was being provided. Although the refugees were not required to attend any meeting or church service, large numbers started attending Sunday services. Due to the limited space available at the church, the decision was taken to start a second service. This service was more evangelistic in nature and was geared to those who were not familiar with Christian vocabulary and forms of worship. Those who had already become followers of Christ would attend the first service, where there was more biblical teaching about the Christian faith and life.

The result of the church being inclusive and showing compassion to those in desperate need was quite unexpected. Besides nominal Christians growing in their faith in Christ, the number of Muslims who turned up in church wanting to know about Jesus and then coming to faith and getting baptized was unprecedented. It had always been assumed that the local church would never be effective in reaching Muslims with the gospel. The impact was also on church members, as many became involved in serving in these ministries of compassion. There was a sense of renewal within the congregation.

A number of discipleship groups using DBS material and other materials were formed. Some focused on evangelism and reaching out to their neighbours, while others were used to train new leaders.

One interesting consequence was that the various Syrian communities began to bond together. Syria is a deeply divided society along religious, ethnic, and political lines. These were evident even in the refugee communities. The refugees quickly learned that the church operates by different values, and these values started to shape their own attitudes and behaviour. As a result, the Syrians started to act as a unified group regardless of their backgrounds and differences.

The members of the church learned how to be tolerant towards Muslims and their traditions. They learned to appreciate the different faith journeys that Muslims take as they grow in their faith in Jesus and came to accept that these disciples would maintain certain cultural practices such as wearing the hijab and fasting during daylight in Ramadan.

Missiological Reflection: Three Strategies and Three Principles (by Rupen Das)

Christian organizations in Lebanon have opted for one of three strategies in addressing social issues. The first is through being an overtly Christian organization or institution that provides social services. The American University of Beirut (AUB) and the hospital attached to it, along with organizations such as World Vision,[9] provide services to the community. These are open to anyone regardless of religion or ethnicity, and there is no conditionality to the assistance that is provided, whether it is education, health services or relief. The organizations identify themselves as Christian – using a broad definition and not limited to any denomination – but are not involved in

---

9. World Vision is a global Christian humanitarian organization, see www.worldvision. org (accessed 11 January 2019).

any kind of spiritual activity such as evangelism, Bible distribution or church planting. They provide a Christian presence in a pluralistic society and, through the work they do and the services they provide, they are able to shape the perception of Christianity and who Christians are. As a result of the quality of their work, they are well regarded and highly respected.

The second strategy is where a group of Christians set up a secular NGO through which they are able to address needs in the community. Knowing the highly sectarian and religiously fragmented nature of Lebanese society, they opt for the secular approach so that their impact would not be limited to any specific religious or ethnic community. This enables them to work in communities where they normally would not have been welcome if they had been identified with a particular religious group. Their motivation is clearly Christian and biblical, and their desire is to demonstrate the compassion of Christ. Many of them work in some of the poorest neighbourhoods and among the most marginalized. By treating the residents as human beings and with dignity, they enable them to encounter and experience the kingdom of God, even if they do not know the King yet.

The third strategy is where Christian NGOs and local churches provide humanitarian assistance or address specific issues regarding poverty or injustice as part of their Christian witness. As Christian communities, they are also involved in a range of spiritual activities such as evangelism, Bible studies and discipleship, church planting and worship. Some see providing assistance as a means to attract people to the gospel message, while others see it as a demonstration of the reality of the kingdom of God. For the latter, the assistance provided is not just a means to an end; rather it is just as valid a ministry as evangelism. Most ensure that there is no conditionality or manipulation in the provision of humanitarian services.

The challenge for the church throughout history has been to find a balance between ensuring that the faith of the community survived and engaging with the world around them in meaningful ways. Jürgen Moltmann, the German theologian at the University of Tübingen, describes the struggle between identity and relevance that the church faces in every generation and in every country. The struggle is for the church to constantly define and protect its identity, which is often shaped by its history, in the midst of competing and changing values in the surrounding cultures, and threats from the political context. Unfortunately, this can cause the church to be inward-looking and thereby lose its relevance. However, the process of remaining true to what it means to be a people of God and followers of Christ, while engaging with the community and finding ways to be relevant, will change the church.[10]

The tensions amongst survival, faithfulness and relevance is still very much at the core of how churches in Syria and Lebanon are engaging with the displacement caused by the Syrian crisis. The existential threats felt by Christians and churches have prompted many of the Catholic and Orthodox churches to provide assistance to their members who have been displaced or are otherwise in need through their denominational relief departments. Some of the Protestant churches, on the other hand, have seen this moment in history as a strategic God-given opportunity to move from the margins of society (being considered latecomers in the social and religious landscape), by becoming places of compassion and having an influence with the gospel within the larger social context.[11]

As the Syrian crisis unfolded and displaced people spilled into Lebanon from 2011 onwards, local agencies like the LSESD decided to respond to the unfolding humanitarian crisis. Being a denomination-based agency, it worked to empower local churches across its denomination in Syria and Lebanon to reach beyond their comfort zones and social boundaries to help those in need with food-aid, emergency supplies, access to health care, water and education, and programmes for children.

What happened as a result is remarkable. Not only did hundreds from all faiths attend participating churches to access the humanitarian services that were being provided, but many asked for prayer, attended church services and Bible studies, and sent their children to Sunday School. The requests for Christian literature outstripped supplies. Other churches and mission agencies reported similar responses. In most situations, there were no conditions imposed to receive assistance, and there was no manipulation.

There are a number of factors which probably contributed to this openness, especially within the Muslim community. In his survey, David Garrison points out that during times of conflict and violence Muslims are very open to the world outside their community.[12] For many Muslim refugees, their contact with Christians had been so limited that they sometimes had warped perceptions. A comment heard at times was, "I never knew that Christians can be kind."

---

10. Jürgen Moltmann, *The Crucified God* (London: SCM Press, 1974), 3.

11. See Nehla Issac, "Syria as a Wakeup for the Syrian Church," in *The Church in Disorienting Times*, Jonathan Andrews, ed. (Carlisle: Langham Global Library, 2018), 68–72.

12. David Garrison, *A Wind in the House of Islam* (Monument: WIGTake Resources, 2014), 244.

Another factor which contributed to this openness was the fact that local evangelical churches did not have elaborate rituals that newcomers had to learn and therefore the barriers for participation were minimized. These churches allowed them to keep their symbols of identity such as the hijab and beards, symbols that had no idolatrous connotations or in any way indicated demonic allegiances. There were very few foreigners involved in the implementation, and the face of the ministries of compassion was Arab, both Syrian and Lebanese. These churches provided extensive pastoral care through prayer, visiting them in their dwellings, enabling some to find jobs, and helping children to get into schools. Finally, and most importantly, local churches provided them with community when their communities had been destroyed.

If local churches are to be involved in ministries of compassion such as relief and development, and in addressing issues of injustice (see the following chapter), there are concepts and guidelines that need to be understood so that the church is not compromised. Through the process of the relief response, LSESD and its partner churches are beginning to understand how local churches can become places of compassion within the community.

First, the local church is an institution in the community: Evangelicals often focus on the church as a spiritual body that is concerned primarily with the after-life. There is no doubt that the church, the Body of Christ, is a link between the physical and spiritual realities. What is not properly understood is the fact that a local church is an institution in the community. It has obligations, as do other institutions, to the community in which it exists. The local church as an institution in the community naturally has visibility, history, credibility and relationships. As a part of the community, it is a natural and logical place from which a relief project can be implemented, as long as there is no conditionality or manipulation in receiving the aid provided.

Second, a local church needs to be a church and not an NGO or a social service organization. Many Christian NGOs and donors that seek to work with and through local churches, unintentionally turn these churches into social service organizations through their operating and management practices, requirements and restrictions. A local church is a worshipping community, with preaching, teaching, discipling, counselling, praying and assisting those in need, "so that the body of Christ may be built up until we all reach unity in the faith and in the knowledge of the Son of God and become mature, attaining to the whole measure of the fullness of Christ" (Eph 4:12–13).

Well-intentioned donors often require churches receiving their funding to not be involved in evangelism, any form of proselytism, or in any other spiritual activity during the period when aid is being provided. This is based on the Code of Conduct for the International Red Cross and Red Crescent Movement, which is widely endorsed.[13] They feel that it would be manipulative because of the power dynamics involved between those providing the aid and the beneficiaries.

The reality is that power dynamics are a part of every human relationship; eliminating them is neither realistic nor possible. However, they can be managed and their impact minimized. The fundamental issue in being able to manage the power dynamic is that there should be no conditionality to the aid as it is being provided, nor should there be manipulation by those providing humanitarian services.

Third, the local church needs to partner with others within the community and beyond while retaining its identity as a church. Local churches have specific roles and functions within a community and many are afraid of losing their distinctive identity if they became active in addressing social needs. Providing assistance to those in need can be intimidating because of the wide range of recipients' needs. The local church needs to be a place of compassion that can connect those with specific needs with other agencies and organizations that have the expertise and resources to help. Many churches will network with other churches but find it difficult to network with service providers and other humanitarian institutions in the community, even when these organizations have similar values.

The emerging phenomenon is that of the local church becoming a place of compassion as part of their witness to the gospel and the kingdom of God. The involvement of the local church allows for a more holistic proclamation and demonstration of the good news of the kingdom of God.

By becoming a place of compassion, the local church is able to proclaim in word and deed God's gracious invitation to his kingdom through Christ. It ensures that the church's interaction with Muslims and other communities is not just verbal and intellectual. It moves beyond the apologetic and the polemic, and integrates life and theology into a wholeness, which our experience in Syria and Lebanon shows that Muslims understand.

---

13. See https://media.ifrc.org/ifrc/who-we-are/the-movement/code-of-conduct/ (accessed 11 December 2018).

5

Engagement for Social Justice in the Mission of God

In this chapter we continue the theme of the implications of being Christ's disciples as we explore how Christianity requires us to confront injustice and be engaged in social justice. The Arab Spring (see glossary), or uprisings, have brought the issues of social justice very much to the forefront of societies across the Middle East.

Our considerations are provided by Robert Hamd (see contributors' bios) assisted by Samah Fakhreldein.

Background: What Is Social Justice? (by Samah Fakhreldein)

Social justice means to have an equal society where all its members are treated justly and equitably. It is where all the members of the society have equal opportunities, with no restrictions based on their group identity, such as gender, religion, ethnicity or national origin.[1]

A report by Jihad Azour for the United Nations in 2014 concerning social justice in the Arab world revealed that discussion about social justice in the media and within think-tank circles had increased dramatically since 2011. This correlates with the Arab Spring. The UN did not refer explicitly to social justice in its founding charter, nor in the *Universal Declaration of Human Rights* (1948) nor the two covenants derived therefrom.[2] However, the UN did refer to

---

1. See for example, A. Jamal Amaney and Michael Robbins, *Social Justice and the Arab Uprisings*, April 2015, http://website.aub.edu.lb/ifi/publications/Documents/working_papers/20150401_sjau.pdf (accessed 9 December 2018).

2. These are the *International Covenant on Civil and Political Rights* and the *International Covenant on Economic, Social and Cultural Rights* which were adopted in 1966.

social development in the *Copenhagen Declaration on Social Development* and the *Programme of Action* adopted by the World Summit for Social Development held in 1995. Azour states on page 2 of his report that:

> the United Nations as a whole makes no explicit distinction between international justice or justice among nationals, and social justice or justice among people. It does tie the concept to economic justice, as that is "hampered by the concentration of wealth and power that seems to accompany the dissemination of the capitalist ethos." The *Department of Economic and Social Affairs* (DESA) of the United Nations goes on to say that social justice is equivalent to distributive justice, as both terms are understood to be interchangeable in common parlance and international relations. DESA also states that the neglect of the pursuit of social justice translates into an acceptance of a future of violence and chaos.[3]

The report presents different opinions about how social justice leads to individual empowerment within social participation, since an individual's decisions are not necessarily dependent on his or her belonging to a particular group. The report concludes that living in social justice is equivalent to living in dignity.

The Arab world suffers from issues relating to social injustice, such as low political freedom, high levels of unemployment, human trafficking, the rising cost of living, large inequalities in wealth, increasing poverty and the social insecurity that results from the lack of the freedom of speech.

Gregor Hamann's report on social justice in North Africa and Middle East entitled *Towards a New Social Contract* defines three factors that can be used to measure social justice in the region: poverty, inequality and defencelessness.[4] Poverty is measured by the average annual income. Inequality from how the resources and income are distributed across the population, and he determines the defencelessness ratio based on participation in public networks.

That is why Azour in his conclusion assures us that:

---

3. Jihad Azour, *Social Justice in the Arab World* (New York: UN, Economic and Social Commission for Western Asia, 2014), 2, www.unescwa.org/sites/www.unescwa.org/files/publications/files/e_escwa_sdd_14_bp-1_e.pdf (accessed 9 December 2018). This source cites DESA, *Social Justice in an Open World: The Role of the United Nations* (New York: UN, 2006), 4, 6.

4. George Hamann, *Towards a New Social Contract: Social Justice in North Africa and Middle East*, September 2011, https://library.fes.de/pdf-files/iez/08475.pdf (accessed 15 December 2018).

Social justice in the Arab world is an aspiration that cannot be realized unless governments recognize the need to implement policies to advance the concept. Policies that provide equitable opportunities to all citizens should be a priority, as investing in human capital can help spur economic growth and bring together different segments of society towards a future of social justice. Unless managed as a holistic transformation agenda (social, economic and political) that emerges from within Arab countries, the ongoing transformation may be protracted and may not meet the aspirations of its citizens.[5]

The Arab Spring brought issues of social justice to the forefront. One major theme was protesting against abusive practices by governments and their neglect of social justice issues, especially economic opportunities, political rights and human rights principles. For instance, in Egypt a common chant was "bread, dignity and social justice," combining the need for basic rights with telling the government that it had failed in fulfilling its duties of providing proper life means with dignity for its people.

A study by Michael Robbins and Amaney Jamal on the topic of social justice and the Arab uprisings concluded that:

> There have been some improvements in perceived levels of equality since the Arab Spring, but vast challenges remain. Although the Arab Spring brought citizens' needs to the forefront, it is imperative that regimes continue to take these demands seriously. Successful reforms to address inequalities will be a lengthy process, but one that is necessary to bring better governance and long-term stability to the region. Above all, regimes must begin by trying to rebuild trust between those who govern and those whom they govern. Redressing this lack of trust – the result of officials not caring for individual needs and building corrupt systems – is necessary to promote more significant reforms. Providing citizens with a greater say in how they are governed is an important first step in this process. Fortunately, many already believe that they can influence their governments. However, channeling this influence through official channels is a key challenge. Currently, it appears likely that most citizens see demonstrations and strikes as the most important means by which to have a say, which promotes instability

---

5. Azour, *Social Justice*, 11.

and uncertainty and can endanger the well-being of those who choose to undertake this potentially dangerous act. Recently, some regimes have provided citizens with a meaningful say in free and fair elections. More should follow the Tunisian example of respecting their outcomes which could lead to improving the prospects for social justice. By creating effective government institutions, for example, regimes could more effectively begin to address the longstanding economic problems that have led to economic stagnation and a lack of opportunities for many citizens, particularly youth. These efforts would help ensure that the gains of the Arab Spring are maintained, and governments in the region take further steps to promote social justice.[6]

Case Studies (by Samah Fakhreldein)

Our case studies in this chapter take us to Egypt and Lebanon. The contrast between rich and poor, honoured and ignored, pervades these stories. Our focus remains on the difference that Christians have brought and their continuing efforts to bring further transformation.

"Bread, Freedom, Social Justice"

This was one of the slogans during Egypt's revolution when President Mubarak resigned on 25 January 2011 (see appendix). It is important to note that bread also means life in Egypt. During the revolution the poor and oppressed came out shouting and protesting, calling for essential rights including bread, freedom and equality. Many faced police bullets: some protesters were killed, others lost an eye or suffered other injuries. Many felt that they had nothing precious to lose, their lives having already been lost under the corrupt regime. Blood was everywhere, its smell mixed with that of gunpowder. People were running and screaming. In the middle of this scene, a huge stage was set up in the biggest square in Cairo, Tahrir Square,[7] where some politicians and religious leaders stood in support of the demonstrators.

The then head of the Coptic Orthodox Church, Pope Shenouda III, warned his people against going out and sharing in demonstrations, stating that "the

---

6. Amaney and Robbins, *Social Justice and the Arab Uprisings*, 23.

7. Literally, Revolution Square, a reference to Egypt's independence from the UK in 1922.

church does not wish to participate in politics." However, an evangelical church located near Tahrir Square acted to support the protestors, using their building as a temporary clinic and with members of their council and worship teams on the stage. In the midst of a crowd of thousands of people, the name of Jesus was proclaimed loudly for all to hear. Furthermore, a church elder stood on the stage teaching the people about their constitutional rights, daring also to speak about Jesus who sets the oppressed free. This man's name is Ehab el-Kharrat.

Ehab (whom we met in chapter 3) is a former youth worker who graduated from the Faculty of Medicine at Cairo University in 1982 before earning a master's degree and doctorate in psychiatry from the University of Kent, UK, specializing in the treatment of addiction. He has been involved in social justice issues for many years as a result of his ministry among drug addicts and those at risk of HIV infection. Moreover, he has established several centres for rehabilitation from various social and psychological addictions. When asked to describe his motivation for political activism, he responded with a smile, "I was influenced by my father, an intellectual and novelist who was himself deeply involved in political life. He raised me to respect freedom and dignity, to pursue social justice and seek the transformation of society."

Ehab has been active in politics since his student days. Initially he received little support from the leaders of his church, although the then senior pastor, Rev Menis Abdelnour, believed him to be a youth leader with a vision for transformation and offered his support. In 1990 he became a member of the Egyptian Organization for Human Rights, and he is a former president of an organization called The World Gathered to Deal with Abuse and Addiction which has members from seventy-five countries. In a culture where honour and shame are highly significant, he chose to stand alongside the ashamed and help them to see themselves as God views them.

When he was asked about the relationship between his ministry and political engagement, specifically how an evangelical church elder might also be both a politician and social worker, he responded that, "when I was young, I used to struggle with this issue for a long time. Then I was introduced to the Lausanne Covenant document,[8] particularly an article by Samuel Escobar on evangelism and the search of man for freedom and dignity, as well as other articles about the importance of social reformation and political involvement. This showed me the relationships amongst systematic theology, religious revival and the importance of advocating for human rights."

---

8. www.lausanne.org/content/covenant/lausanne-covenant (accessed 13 December 2018).

Ehab adopted these values as his own, believing that social justice is accomplished hand in hand through both political and social transformation. He was involved in both the 2011 and 2013 Egyptian revolutions (see appendix). He was one of the five founders of the Egyptian Social Democratic Party and became a member of the Shura (literally, consultancy), the Upper House of Parliament. He remains politically active in the promotion of freedom and dignity for all Egyptians.

"Blessed Are the Merciful, for They Will Be Shown Mercy" (Matt 5:7)

When you visit the suburb of Hay el Gharbeh in southern Beirut for the first time, you will understand why many refer to Lebanon as "a land of diversity and contradiction." Living in extreme poverty, the people of Hay el Gharbeh are socially and economically isolated from mainstream Lebanese society. The neighbourhood became a settlement for the Dom community (see glossary) during the fifteen-year civil war (see appendix) along with Lebanese families displaced from the south and the Palestinians already present there since 1948 (the Shatila camp is adjacent to Hay el Gharbeh, itself an area of severe poverty and injustice). The Dom is a community largely overlooked by mainstream Lebanese society and politics. When you walk through its dusty narrow streets in the shadows of Beirut's massive sports arena and see the small cement rooms and naked, unbathed children running about, mostly barefoot, you cannot help but be overwhelmed by the contradictions in Lebanese society.[9]

Tahaddi ("Challenge" in Arabic) is an organization in Hay el Gharbeh whose mission is to confront the challenge of poverty.[10] Tahaddi was established to fill the gap created by the injustice faced by the Dom community as a result of their social exclusion. Tahaddi's work was started in the 1990s by Dr Agnès Sanders, a French physician, and Catherine Mortada, a Syrian-Swiss educator. Agnès and Catherine used to walk in the dust and mud of Hay el Gharbeh offering what assistance they could. They would sit with the families and drink traditional coffee offered to welcome guests. With time, the two women earned the trust of the community and came to know intimately the extreme poverty and vulnerability pervading the neighbourhood. They noticed that the main needs of the community were health and education, which matched their professional expertise.

---

9. Rupen Das and Julie Davidson, *Profiles of Poverty: The Human Face of Poverty in Lebanon* (Beirut: Dar Manhal al Hayat, 2011), 267.

10. www.tahaddilebanon.org/ (accessed 26 April 2018).

Catherine explained how they started by simply renting a place in the area. "We did not have anything in mind as a specific Tahaddi project at that time. We were introduced to this area by a friend who found a shelter in the sports city which was bombed during the civil war."

They were driven by the sense of concern for the children who did not have access to schooling in this marginalized area. Driven by the parable of the Good Samaritan (Luke 10:25–37), Catherine believed that the ministry of Tahaddi, along with its dedicated and diverse on-site staff team, was a response to Jesus's call for compassion towards our neighbour, whoever they might be. She also recognized what they did as being a small mustard seed of God's kingdom which would help the families of Hay el Gharbeh find both freedom from oppression and fresh opportunities.

In response to a question regarding her motivations behind devoting her life to this kind of work, Catherine replied that, "we do what Jesus himself would be humbly doing – going to people to whom few would go. We demonstrate in a practical way the love of God reflected in Jesus, who himself cared for the uncared and fought injustice and discrimination. We provide education or health care in a holistic way by showing hospitality for the poor and sick regardless of their social background, religion, or denomination."

With time, they found permanent buildings in the neighbourhood and opened two centres to house Tahaddi's expanding activities: a community health centre, which provides basic health care services for families; and a learning centre, which provides education for children too old to access the Lebanese school system or for those who dropped out.

In 2008, Tahaddi was officially registered as a non-profit organization. They are independent and have no political affiliations. Moreover, they serve socially vulnerable families and victims of conflict and discrimination, regardless of their nationality, religion and social background. Having begun with two women, by 2018 Tahaddi had become a committed team of approximately fifty people of diverse backgrounds with daily operations serving the community in line with their three core values of compassion, justice and empowerment.

What makes someone like Catherine spend her life working in Hay el Gharbeh when she could have had a secure life in Switzerland? Catherine, a daughter of a Syrian father and a Swiss mother, lived in Switzerland until the age of twenty-nine. She also felt she belonged to the Middle East, and she wanted to share her skills which is why she moved to Lebanon. Catherine began by teaching French in the half-destroyed school of Notre Dame de la Paix in 1990, located in a very poor area of Beirut. She started to visit women in prison and continued to do so for fifteen years, joined later by Agnès, caring more specifically, but not exclusively, for migrant workers. Working in prison and in Hay el Gharbeh has deepened her faith and taught her humility through resilience and the faith she has seen in so many around her in difficult situations and sometimes dire poverty. For her, Tahaddi is not simply an education centre or a medical centre – it is a voice for the voiceless.[11] It is an initiative designed to help marginalized populations (the Dom people but also the displaced and very poor) access their rights to education and proper medical care, which they have been denied for too long. It is a way to tell them that they are to be respected and not dispossessed.

The Philemon Project – Creating a Human Being

"The church is not a charitable organization!" This was one church's response to the case of a mother, an Ethiopian, who knew that her child had been tied with a rope in the day-care centre while she was at work.

Rev Robert Hamd's doctoral dissertation looked at the church's self-understanding of the *missio Dei* as seen through the lens of working with the very poor. He focused on how the church views migrant domestic workers and the *kafala* system (see glossary). Robert analyzed how fifty clergy in Lebanon understood how the church could bring about or inspire social and ethical change. What he found was that "the church often pulled away from, rather than confronting, these issues. The church focused on protecting its own people and community."

Robert was raised by Lebanese Druze parents who emigrated to USA to find a better life for their family during the Lebanese Civil War (see appendix). He describes his parents as "hidden immigrants" who "lived in USA, but their own Lebanese Druze culture remained untouched." At the age of twelve, Robert was invited to a church summer camp, where he heard the gospel for the first time. It was there, too, that he received a missionary call, having what he describes as a profound religious experience. He clarified, "God needed to get my attention in a profound way. I had a burning desire to know Jesus and, throughout the camp, I kept hearing the word missionary. I asked my friend if he had heard anything, but he had not. At the time, I had never heard the word missionary before, so I asked my counsellors about its meaning. They defined it as someone who bears witness for Christ wherever they are, and someone who crosses cultures to do so."

---

11. Compare Proverbs 31:8a, "Speak up for those who cannot speak for themselves."

It was not until Robert visited Lebanon again at the age of sixteen that he again tried to make sense of this, and it was at the age of twenty-one that he decided to follow Jesus completely. Accordingly, he was rejected from his family, a moment that causes him distress, conflict and struggle to this day. He declared, "following Christ cost me my family support, but I have no regrets."

Robert sees his call for the marginalized as rooted in Isaiah 58:10: "And if you spend yourselves on behalf of the hungry, and satisfy the needs of the oppressed, then your light will rise in the darkness, and your night will become like the noonday." He realized that the gospel is not about proclamation only: it is about the whole human being, and there is a social side to Jesus's message. Eschewing ostentation, he sees a real model in Mother Teresa's life and ministry and considers his ministry to be about less of him and more of Christ.

In Lebanon, Robert began to think about how the ministry of the local church could be reframed in such a way as to convey its message to those beyond its walls. He had found the church was disengaged from the poor. They may donate money for them, but otherwise remained distant.

A particularly tragic, yet unfortunately all-too-common, incident involved a domestic worker who had been repeatedly raped by her employer. With a lack of professional oversight or legal protections, many domestic service workers in the Middle East can exist in almost slave-like conditions, subject to exploitation and abuse. After running away from the home, she found out she was pregnant and as a result wanted to commit suicide. According to Robert:

> we found her, and she wanted us to assist her to have an abortion. Ethically, we could not; instead, we walked alongside her through the process of giving birth. When she wanted to work she had difficulty finding a proper place for the baby. She eventually located a low-cost centre for poor children. However, it was being operated illegally by unqualified people. One malpractice that she discovered was that they tied the children to chairs. When our Ethiopian friend showed us pictures of this, we immediately confronted the church about the need to intervene and about the need for creating the Philemon Project.

The project provides a learning centre for the very poor, focusing on neglected children from the ages of one to four. Children are welcomed from any social, political or religious background. Robert said they help children understand the rules of engagement with society, adding "you could call it 'creating a human being.'"

Missiological Reflection: For the Least of These (by Robert Hamd)

The term social justice can mean many things to different people. Daniel G. Groody suggests that "justice means everything and nothing."[12] For some, justice implies protest and resistance. For others, justice means fairness, the rule of law or trying to make right an egregious violation. Still others understand justice to be a cosmic court, where a wronged victim has their day of reckoning. Nevertheless, for the church, justice takes on particular importance, informed by Scriptures that recognize all people as made in the image of God, which requires that they be treated with dignity, self-worth and freedom from exploitation within a social order.

The concept of social order denotes community, collective group, or a constellation of human beings brought together through social forms, which includes culture, religion, economics, the rule of law and language. These social forms are best understood as the factors that, in coming together, create societal order.

We will be looking at social justice from a Christian theological viewpoint. Broadly speaking, religion provides meaning for life. Religion provides ecclesial structures, and most importantly, according to sociologist Émile Durkheim, it reinforces the morals and social norms held collectively within a society.[13]

Turning our attention to the Scriptures, particularly the Old Testament, Horst Dietrich Preuss provides a view relevant to our discussion. When we talk about Israel, the biblical texts speak of community, denoted by "we" and "us" references, recognizing Israel as a social community held together by language, culture and sacred rites. Preuss adds that "Israel" can also mean an individual when referred to as "I" in the Old Testament (e.g. Gen 32:28).[14] Thus, the Old Testament understands social order to encompass both community and personal obligations interchangeably. It is important in our discussion to distinguish both the communal and individual implications of Scripture.

Daniel G. Groody defines justice as having two elements, internal and external. He believes internal justice "deals with one's experience of justification" or salvation in Jesus Christ.[15] By this definition, we can explain justification as

---

12. Daniel G. Groody, *Globalization, Spirituality, and Justice: Navigating the Path to Peace, Theology in Global Context* (Maryknoll: Orbis Books, 2007), 26.

13. Émile Durkheim, *The Elementary Forms of Religious Life* (New York: Free Pr., 1995), 198.

14. Horst Dietrich Preuss, *Old Testament Theology*, vol. 1, Old Testament Library (Louisville: Westminster/John Knox Press, 1995), 60. See also Yohanna Katanacho, *The Land of Christ* (Nazareth: self-published, 2012), 42–46.

15. Groody, *Globalization, Spirituality*, 26.

an event whereby a person is declared to be in a right relationship with God through the saving work of Jesus (Gal 2:15–16; Rom 5:1). Thus, internal justice is explicitly linked to redemption. New Testament scholar George Eldon Ladd contends the Gospels announced that Jesus brought to lost sinners a new experience of forgiveness. He did not tell the woman in the house of Simon that God was forgiving her or explaining to her the way she might find salvation; he pronounced, "Your sins are forgiven" (Luke 7:48).[16] In the New Testament, the example of those who received internal justification or redemption set Jesus's followers on a new trajectory, that of demonstrating forgiveness received by outwardly manifesting ethical acts of love. Thus, Jesus calls his new community, and by extension all Christians, to "thirst for righteousness, for they will be filled" (Matt 5:3). The Greek word *dikaiosuné* translated as righteousness can also be translated as justice or justness. In other words, Jesus alone can forgive sins and call his followers to practical righteousness as a continuation of his mission.

This outward, or external, expression of justice is a result of this inward work of God. If Jesus is Saviour for Christians, how might their personal, internal justification be the principal motivator to lead Christians to visible works of social justice? I argue that internal justice compels Christians to love the Lord God with all their heart, soul, and mind, but then this love should move the community to external acts of justice and love for their neighbour as themselves (Matt 22:37–39).

The Old Testament provides a helpful framework to understand external justice and its place within the community. The community was called to right relationships with neighbours. For example, when the Old Testament talks about justice, it speaks about two variations: *sedaqah*, used 523 times to convey "righteousness" and *mishpat*, used 422 times referring to "justice of judgment."[17] Furthermore, Christopher J. H. Wright argues that *Yhwh* (God) entrusts his people to be *sedaqah*, calling the community to be a light to the nations.[18]

Thus, Jesus demonstrates a missiology informed by the law of love. Jesus always pushes our understanding of the love of God and then invites us to extend it missiologically to love of neighbour. First-century hearers were well acquainted with love for neighbour, but that love was restricted to the people

---

16. George Eldon Ladd, *A Theology of the New Testament* (Grand Rapids: Eerdmans, 1993), 77.

17. Groody, *Globalization, Spirituality*, 27.

18. Christopher J. H. Wright, *The Mission of God's People: A Biblical Theology of the Church's Mission* (Grand Rapids: Zondervan, 2010), 90.

of God (Lev 19:18).[19] Jesus sets the tone for our social justice discovery by crossing barriers to model the mission of God as including any person in need (Luke 10:29–37).

Concerning social justice, we are called, therefore, to practise right relationships with our neighbours. To have right relationships, our communities must engage in external (*mishpat*) justice. As we move forward in our investigation, we should recognize how the Bible expresses the larger narrative that God is a missionary. God is committed to crossing boundaries to reconcile the world.[20] In addition, social justice as mission is framed, for God's people, on a love for God that includes a love for neighbours. Practically speaking, the church must grapple with faithfully bearing witness to Christ by struggling to make relationships right with individuals, families, neighbours and the wider world.

We can find many critiques in the debate over evangelism versus social action. This discussion has plagued the church for a long time. Indeed, we experience daily challenges from the many Christians who do not affirm the need for social justice work. Yet Christians have founded schools, hospitals and orphanages, to name only a few spheres of engagement with social needs. The tension lies in where we place our emphasis – on proclamation or social justice? Or can it be both?

David Bosch provides a helpful argument: that God's mission is for the "church to step out of itself, into the wider world." He reminds us that stepping out of ourselves is vital and demonstrates that we rightly comprehend the essence of the gospel. Namely, that justice is God's very character, and God sent his Son into the world to save a world mired by catastrophic sin. Bosch argues that the "heart of mission" is evangelism, or proclaiming Christ. Proclamation is based on love, which contains two important components – word and deed.[21] For Bosch, when Christians engage in mission, they have decided to cross over boundaries, an action that results in a humble reliance on God while seeking to be transformative by demonstrating God's mission in a holistic manner.

Christopher J. H. Wright takes the argument a step further, arguing that the whole meta-narrative of the Scriptures is a story of God's engagement with the world, through God's people, for the ultimate purpose of the redemption

---

19. Ladd, *Theology of the New Testament*, 131.

20. Wright, *Mission of God's People*, 28.

21. David J. Bosch, "Evangelism: Theological Currents and Cross-Currents Today," *International Bulletin of Missionary Research* 11, no. 3 (1987): 100–101.

of all God's creation.[22] According to Wright, the grand narrative of the Bible is understood from a missiological reading of biblical theology.

The church needs to be intentional in its interaction with its societal context. Our missional engagement needs to be deliberate, to bear witness to God's gracious and merciful nature through engagement in social justice. Bearing witness in social justice is crucial and cannot be argued away because the stakes are so high for people who suffer from injustices – in reality, it is a life and death matter of human misery. Our social action provides a point of contact with our context. Often, our practises are interpreted by the community as following our Lord's example as welcoming strangers, aliens, the weak, the poor and the refugee, and making them feel at home.

There are a number of practical aspects that are worth mentioning. First, to be clear in the scope of what one is attempting. When we limit and describe what we can and cannot do, we build on our strengths and identify critical areas of need: those pressing issues in our context requiring our attention to tackling the social justice concerns. The temptation to attempt to solve all social problems can fatigue our volunteer base, our resources and our emotional capacity to carry out our tasks over an extended period. We increase the chances of completing the task we sense that God is calling us to undertake by clearly defining the scope of our project. We are then in a better position to be more effective, we will be less likely to be side-tracked, and we increase the chances of providing a high-quality service.

The second aspect is the need to develop our expertise. This flows from and dovetails with being clear about the scope. Internal technical expertise focuses on developing organization skills, and know-how to achieve valid results. External expertise gives our work the capacity to serve others in holistic and tangible ways. By providing relief, development and justice, we help create homeostasis[23] in communities and build strategy structures for transformational and lasting change.

The third aspect is the importance of working with others. (Several aspects of doing this were discussed in the previous chapter.)

Returning to the biblical text and the story of salvation history, the archetype of both proclamation and social justice engagement is Jesus.

Born in a stable in Bethlehem, Jesus grows, lives, and works in Galilee (Mark 1:16). Jesus's place of birth and Galilee location are more than a geographical

---

22. Wright, *Mission of God's People*, 532–533.

23. A biological term for the state of steady internal conditions maintained by living things, a dynamic balance of multiple variables that seeks to maintain optimal conditions for living.

accident.[24] It signifies Jesus's origin among the poor and excluded. J. Andrew Kirk notes that the words and actions of Jesus recorded in Luke 4:18–19 caused bewilderment and astonishment among the crowds that followed him.[25] On numerous occasions, Jesus's closest disciples misunderstood what was going on since it demonstrated God's favour beyond and outside of Israel.[26]

Jesus informs our missiological engagement through his deeds. Jesus crossed boundaries and sought contact with the excluded. His relationship with the marginalized expressed kingdom ethics. Jesus had table fellowship with Samaritans, tax collectors, the sick and the sinful; all the excluded of society. He was with the weak, such as women and children, and radically taught about forgiveness (Matt 18:21–35) and a love for enemies (Luke 6:27–36). His numerous healings recorded in the Gospels point to "God's desire to bring about the healing of the nations."[27]

Social justice is practical and takes on progressive forms, as the context demands. Jesus's ministry demonstrates how important human relationships are, calling us to give our time, money and energies into correcting social injustices for the poor, excluded and outsider. Thus, the life of Jesus provides us a consistent framework to measure our social justice engagement. Through his life, ministry, death and resurrection we see a divine movement of God moving to the poor, the alien and the disenfranchised. We learn that Jesus does not limit his care and grace to his community, but rather expands grace to include all peoples with whom he comes into contact.

The apostle Paul reminds us, "for he himself is our peace, who made the two groups one and has destroyed the barrier, the dividing wall of hostility, by setting aside in his flesh the law with its commands and regulations" (Eph 2:14–15). Our social justice engagement is only as effective as combining it with making Jesus known to those we are called to serve lovingly. Nevertheless, making Jesus's love known is a huge endeavour, which concerns the whole person for each human being. Therefore, we embrace social justice ministries as a valid means to demonstrate the multifaceted love of God in Christ to our context. We recognize that no one approach addresses all circumstances satisfactorily. Thus, we believe Jesus alone provides us with the framework

---

24. Groody, *Globalization, Spirituality*, 48–49.

25. "Preach the good news to the poor, to proclaim release to the captives, to give sight to the blind, to let the oppressed go free and to proclaim the year of the Lord's favour" (Luke 4:18–19 quoting Isa 61:1–2a).

26. J. Andrew Kirk, *The Church and the World: Understanding the Relevance of Mission* (Milton Keynes: Paternoster, 2014), 52–53.

27. Kirk, *Church and the World*, 54.

to evaluate our social justice engagement, which ultimately calls us to break down the wall that divides people and reconcile the world to himself through his death on the cross.

Therefore, social justice as mission means that churches must be faithful witnesses to the *missio Dei* in their contexts by investing their experience and resources in social justice activities which confront systemic socio-economic injustices. From our context in Lebanon, these systemic socio-economic inequalities affect at-risk communities in destructive ways. Having the theological and emotional courage to challenge systemic problems, says missiologist J. Andrew Kirk, begins with recognizing that God is a God of justice. Kirk points out that God creates humans in his likeness (*imago Dei*), which should inspire us as his followers to take social risks for the disadvantaged.[28]

The Gospels provide for us by interpreting the mission of Jesus into our present context through the lens of Jesus's life and ministry. When we engage in social justice ministries, we are carrying on the ministry which Jesus demonstrated by caring for the poor, confronting injustices and healing the sick. In Mark's Gospel, the writer understands the mission of Jesus as calling his followers to imitate what Jesus has done. As Jesus says in Mark 8:34, "Whoever wants to be my disciple must deny themselves and take up their cross and follow me." For Mark, "to follow" relates not so much to corporally following the crowd around Jesus as it does to emulating what Jesus did as an obedient disciple.

The Philemon Project described above demonstrates my point. It has focused since its inception on providing the best early childhood learning centre and adult mentoring programmes for the communities it serves. We carry out our professional practice with the utmost attention to exceeding early cognitive development benchmarks. We work with whole families to help create transformative impulses without obliging them to consider becoming Christians. We believe our work speaks missiologically.

During the first five years of The Philemon Project we conducted intake and exit interviews with the parents of the children who attended. We paid particular attention to our female participants and their answers. Specifically, Muslim female participants were asked "why do these people do what they do?" In their response, 86 percent of such people linked our work to "doing what Jesus would do." This data bears witness to the significant self-understanding

---

28. J. Andrew Kirk, *What Is Mission?: Theological Explorations* (Minneapolis: Fortress Press, 2000), 98, 103–104.

from our participants about the role social justice plays in mission. The purpose of social justice is never to be used as a means of proselytizing people in need. Nevertheless, knowing that 86 percent of recipients are aware that our social justice work has links to Jesus and his ministry encourages us to argue for an earnest consideration of engagement in social justice as a legitimate expression of the mission of the church.

Land rights.
Identificatan cedulas.
Schooling + literacy.
Medical work.
Development of craft work (chairs - Siwar).
Iniciativa Cristiana
Asociana Anglicana

Radio Antena.
Support for patients (Cristina) + students.
Music + instruments.

6

Christian-Muslim Dialogue in the Mission of God

Our subject in this chapter arises from the previous one: if we are to become engaged in society, then that will inevitably mean speaking with those of other faiths. What is our attitude towards such people, and how does this influence how we relate to them? Can we be friends when we – and those we are speaking with – realize that the others are settled in their religious beliefs and will not convert?

Our examination of this subject is led by three Lebanese people, Martin Accad is joined by Brent Hamoud and Suzie Lahoud (see contributors' bios). Lebanon's history together with the ethnic and religious diversity of its people makes such dialogue inevitable. What might "best practice" look like? And how does the Bible assist us in being faithful in testimony and witness whoever we are speaking with?

Background: A Survey of Christian-Muslim Dialogue in Lebanon (by Brent Hamoud)

Like no other country in the MENA region, Lebanon presents both the wealth of opportunities and breadth of challenges of developing Interfaith Dialogue (IFD). Throughout its rich heritage of diversity – there exist eighteen official religious sects – peaceful coexistence has mixed with flares of religious and sectarian violence to produce a complicated national experience. IFD "has been a reality . . . of daily life since the country's creation," though formal dialogue activities began taking root in the 1970s and 1980s with sporadic, informal activities, oftentimes taking place outside of Lebanon for security reasons.[1] Dialogue efforts increased substantially in the 1990s following the official end of the fifteen-year gruesome civil war (see appendix). Interfaith initiatives were considered a means to promote a common national identity, organize relations between religious communities and create a platform for theological reflection.[2] Leading dialogue participant Mohammad Sammak comments on the state of Lebanon in that post-war period by noting that, although there was a process for a political peace between sectarian groups, "nothing was being done to bring unity and promote cultural reconciliation."[3] Attitudes among many religious leaders and lay people alike continued to evolve so that "where dialogue in Lebanon was once considered non-acceptable, now dialogue is proposed as a necessity."[4]

IFD in Lebanon has largely been characterized as a "Christian initiative especially supported and directed by churches"[5] and much evidence demonstrates the way Christians have taken to engage with other faiths via encounters of dialogue. Even during the outset of war in the mid-1970s, the Middle East Council of Churches (MECC) was organizing interfaith initiatives including joint youth meetings and cooperative relief efforts.[6] Additionally, a number of Christian universities, such as St Joseph (Roman Catholic) and Balamand (*Rum* Orthodox; see glossary), have established educational centres in Christian-Muslim studies.[7] The experience has not been a one-sided affair, however; and willing dialogue partners have emerged across all sectarian lines.

Lebanon's most official expression of IFD has taken shape in the form of the National Committee for Islamic-Christian Dialogue. This body emerged out of a 1993 interfaith "spiritual summit" and consists of a seven-member committee of representatives from various religious backgrounds. Though it does not receive direct support from the government, it is considered "the only group that officially represents the leaders of the different religious and

---

1. Mohammad Abu-Nimer, Amal I. Khoury, and Emily Welty, *Unity in Diversity: Interfaith Dialogue in the Middle East* (Washington DC: United States Institute of Peace, 2007), 103–104.

2. Heidi Hirvonen, *Christian-Muslim Dialogue: Perspectives of Four Lebanese Thinkers* (Leiden, Netherlands: Koninklijke Brill NV, 2013), 3.

3. Mohammad Sammak, "Building Bridges through Interfaith Dialogue," interviewed by Fatiha Kaoues, published in "Reconciliation, Reform and Resilience: Positive Peace for Lebanon," *Accord* 24 (2012): 27. Available at: http://www.c-r.org/sites/default/files/Accord24_Lebanon_ENG.pdf (accessed 22 December 2014).

4. John J. Donohue, *Muslim-Christian Relations: Dialogue in Lebanon*, Occasional Papers Series (Washington DC: Center for Muslim-Christian Understanding, History and International Affairs, Georgetown University, 1996), 4.

5. Abu-Nimer, Khoury, and Welty, *Unity in Diversity*, 102.

6. Abu-Nimer, Khoury, and Welty, 112–113.

7. Abu-Nimer, Khoury, and Welty, 120, 124.

sectarian communities in the country."[8] The creation of such a council was instrumental in changing the view of interfaith participation within Lebanon's volatile sectarian context by presenting dialogue as an avenue for communities to promote common interests rather than a "betrayal to their own group" as it had often been perceived.[9] Another significant development was the creation in 1995 of The Arab Working Group on Muslim-Christian Dialogue (AWGMCD), which materialized when a group of religious leaders from throughout the region gathered in Beirut under the facilitation of the MECC in an effort to translate shared personal convictions into a structured approach to dialogue. A valuable fruit of this venture has been the production of *Dialogue and Coexistence: An Arab Muslim-Christian Covenant*, a document that aims "to articulate principles and broad guidelines which might help give wider currency to the culture of dialogue, mutual understanding, coexistence and common action."[10]

Conservative evangelical Christians in Lebanon have widely demonstrated an indifferent attitude towards IFD. John Azumah's assessment of global evangelicalism in 2012 can aptly be applied to Lebanon when he says, "a significant portion of what might be termed *conservative evangelicals* remain suspicious and scathing about interfaith dialogue in general and dialogue with Muslims in particular."[11] Even so, Protestants – officially referred to as evangelicals in Lebanon – have been among the voices shaping IFD movements within Lebanon. Among these is the Rev Riad Jarjour who served as the general secretary of the MECC from 1994 to 2003 and oversaw increased dialogue efforts. He currently serves as general secretary for the aforementioned AWGMCD. Another evangelical interfaith initiative has been the Institute of Middle East Studies (IMES), which was established in 2003 at the Arab Baptist Theological Seminary (ABTS), which works to "bring about positive transformation in thinking and practice between Christians and Muslims in the Middle East and beyond."[12] Such a programme demonstrates the evolving evangelical attitude that Azumah calls a "moving away from indifferent and

---

8. Abu-Nimer, Khoury, and Welty, 104.

9. Abu-Nimer, Khoury, and Welty, 104.

10. Arab Group for Muslim-Christian Dialogue, *Dialogue and Coexistence: An Arab Muslim-Christian Covenant*, 2001, available at: http://www.agmcd.org/files/covenant.htm (accessed 17 December 2014).

11. John Azumah, "Evangelical Christian Views and Attitudes Towards Christian-Muslim Dialogue," *Transformation* 29, no. 2 (2012): 129.

12. Arab Baptist Theological Seminary, *Institute of Middle East Studies*, available at: www.abtslebanon.org/imes (accessed 21 December 2014).

very negative attitudes to an emerging openness and engagement in dialogue with other religions."[13]

IFD approaches in Lebanon can be characterized by four primary models. One is *dialogue of life* that seeks to foster the shared life experiences among individuals rather than simply the traditional interactions between religious leadership.[14] This approach is what Jarjour calls a "move of dialogue from the top of the hierarchy and the cultural elite to the grassroots level,"[15] and it has been found to be particularly effective among youth and students.[16] A second model, *unity dialogue*, focuses "on the solidarity and unity of Muslims and Christians in the face of shared problems locally, regionally, or internationally."[17] An example of such is a 1996 dialogue initiative by the AWGMCD entitled "Muslims and Christians Together for Jerusalem's Sake."[18] A third model is *ritualistic and ceremonial interfaith dialogue* which promotes shared celebration and participation in religious traditions, such as sharing in a prayer session or jointly observing a ceremony. A most notable example of this approach is the inauguration in 2010 of 25 March as a national interfaith holiday by the Lebanese government. The date commemorates the angel's annunciation of the birth of Jesus to Mary, and it is now celebrated annually through a large interfaith gathering during which passages about Mary and Jesus's birth in both the Bible and the Qur'an are read. This was achieved through the joint efforts of a number of Lebanese religious leaders, both Muslim and Christian.[19] Fourthly, *advocacy approach* applies a "dialogue through action" by building interfaith engagement through development projects in which Christians and Muslims "can get to know each other while working together toward a common goal."[20]

These four models do not capture all the forms in which IFD manifests itself in Lebanon, but they do demonstrate the ways dialogue efforts extend from theoretical conceptions to actual interface of religious communities.

---

13. Azumah, "Evangelical Christian Views," 136.

14. Abu-Nimer, Khoury, and Welty, *Unity in Diversity*, 127.

15. Riad Jarjour, "The Future of Dialogue among People of Faith." *Danish-Arab Interfaith Dialogue*, 11 December 2013, available at: http://danisharabdialogue.org/articles/the-future-of-dialogue-among-people-of-faith?context=category-Articles+in+English (accessed 17 December 2014).

16. Abu-Nimer, Khoury, and Welty, *Unity in Diversity*, 106.

17. Abu-Nimer, Khoury, and Welty, 127.

18. Riad Jarjour, "Text of the Covenant: Preface," *Arab Group for Muslim-Christian Dialogue*, available at: http://www.agmcd.org/files/preface.htm (accessed 16 December 2014).

19. See for example the announcement of this celebration at: http://www.westminsterinterfaith.org.uk/WIN/win66/66_05a_Lebanon.html (accessed 26 September 2016).

20. Abu-Nimer, Khoury, and Welty, *Unity in Diversity*, 127.

IFD initiatives in Lebanon continue to gain momentum as growing numbers of individuals and groups, both local and international, recognize the potential for dialogue to address root challenges facing the country and region. The experience has faced many obstacles and setbacks but "what is positive is that dialogue has become fashionable and the will to dialogue is apparently serious."[21]

Case Studies: The Institute of Middle East Studies – A Prophetic Voice in Muslim- Christian Relations (by Suzie Lahoud)

In this chapter our three case studies are all taken from one organization influencing Christian communities across the Middle East and North Africa from its operational base in Lebanon. Our journey of exploration begins with a quote from Walter Brueggemann.

> "The task of prophetic ministry is to nurture, nourish, and evoke a consciousness and perception alternative to the consciousness and perception of the dominant culture around us."[22]

Elie Haddad, the president of the Arab Baptist Theological Seminary in Beirut, describes the history of Muslim-Christian relations in Lebanon. He reflects on the distance and animosity that existed between these communities, particularly the fallout from the Lebanese Civil War, and how fear created an insular theology of survival in the local church. "We grew up in Lebanon basically hating Muslims, or not caring about them. Even though I grew up in a Muslim neighbourhood in Saida . . . and the majority of my classmates were Muslims, but yet, we never had relationships with Muslims – we did not go to their homes, they did not come to my home . . . So, I did not grow up comfortable being around Muslims."

Dr Martin Accad, a professor at ABTS and the founder of the Institute of Middle East Studies (IMES), likewise refers to the civil war as having been formative in his involvement in Muslim-Christian relations: "I grew up through the civil war; so maybe that is an important piece of the background of why I

---

21. Donohue, *Muslim-Christian Relations*, 20.

22. Walter Brueggemann, *The Prophetic Imagination*, 2nd ed. (Minneapolis: Fortress Press, 2001).

am involved in interfaith relations. I have experienced while growing up what religions can do in terms of conflict."

The birth of IMES is a powerful story of learning to embrace the other. IMES was officially founded in 2003 and is now one of two departments within the seminary. In reflecting on IMES's impact over the years, Accad shares: "I think one significant element of IMES being a part of ABTS is that IMES transformed us before even beginning to transform anybody else." IMES has taken on a life of its own and has infiltrated the lives of many, planting seeds of change in communities across the region and across the world. While those involved feel that its achievements as a catalyst for such positive transformation are still quite modest, this holy dissatisfaction is perhaps also the mark of a truly prophetic ministry.

A Tale of Two Theologians: The Sheikh and His Companion

Sheikh Mohammad Abu Zeid, the head judge of the Sunni court of Saida, and Dr Martin Accad have forged a genuine friendship that has influenced the perceptions of many. The two were first introduced by a mutual friend in 2007 when Dr Martin asked Sheikh Mohammad to speak at a conference on the topic of Women in Islam. "I think I did well then," jokes Sheikh Mohammad. "Dr Martin kept contacting me, and we did two things: either I was inviting him and the students to my city, Saida, usually on Fridays to witness the Friday prayers, and also to visit the city, to know the people; or I was at ABTS in the class to talk about certain issues or topics chosen by Martin. And then year after year I was a speaker at the Middle East Consultation organized by IMES.[23] In 2011 I received a coach load of conference participants in Saida."

After receiving his undergraduate degree in traditional Islamic Law, Sheikh Mohammad went on to study Modern Islamic Thought before enrolling in the Institute of Christian and Islamic Studies at the University of St Joseph. He describes the latter as a sort of cultural exchange programme between his Islamic Institute and the University of St Joseph. Similarly, Martin, having completed his masters' degree at the University of Oxford in Eastern Christianity, wrote his doctoral dissertation on the history of Muslim-Christian relations and dialogue between the eighth and fourteenth centuries. It was out of a common vision that this close friendship and collaboration was born.

---

23. This is an annual consultation. The proceedings of the 2017 event were published in book form; Jonathan Andrews, ed, *The Church in Disorienting Times: Leading Prophetically through Adversity* (Carlisle: Langham Publishing, 2018).

In January 2014 the two theologians travelled together to the United States having been invited by World Vision to attend the annual National Prayer Breakfast in Washington, DC. Accad describes the experience of journeying together for twenty hours and giving lectures at think-tanks and other events as "priceless and really quite unique." A month later Sheikh Mohammad called Dr Martin to say, "I have written a book about our experience together in America. I would like to send it to you so you give me your opinion, because you are one of the main characters." The significance of the title, *The America that I Have Seen*, was not lost on Martin. It is the same as an earlier book written by Sayyid Qutb, the most influential ideologue of the Muslim Brotherhood and one of the founding fathers of modern Islamism. Qutb penned his polemical book based on his disgust at what he observed of American people, society and government whilst living and working in the USA from 1948 to 1950. Sheikh Mohammad describes how he had been very much influenced by the writings of Qutb, and for this reason had been apprehensive at first about his trip to America. However, he noted that he and his Christian companion were both well hosted and received as a positive model for Muslim-Christian relations. "And if Sayyid Qutb went on to the extreme maybe, in a negative way," he adds with a smile, "I think I went to the extreme in a positive way."

The way Sheikh Mohammad communicated his experience of the US is consistent with IMES's approach. "I talked about the American individual. I am not concerned with the policies, nor with the government issues. I am concerned with the people." While neither he nor Martin shy away from political issues, they both choose to emphasize the human aspect of every interaction. Martin often says that "there is a human face behind every movement." This personal connection is what breaks down barriers and allows us to see the other as more like us than we could have ever imagined. It is much more difficult to demonize the enemy that you know, and in knowing, we often discover that they are not the enemy at all. Both theologians – the Sunni Sheikh, and the evangelical Seminary Professor – have discovered, experienced, and been personally transformed by the power of this "knowing," and it is a power that they wield together for the benefit of their communities, while also seeking to positively influence their region and the world.

A Tale of Two Students: That They May Be like Us, or That They May Remain?

George and Eman[24] are both from Egypt but they come from two very distinct communities. He was born a Christian; she, a Muslim. For George, Islam had

---

24. Both names have been changed to protect their identities.

always been something to defend oneself against and to dismantle. In his zeal to be a faithful witness to Jesus Christ, he would often take part in religious chat rooms, debating with Muslims over the true doctrines of Christianity. "I felt that a Christian could not have a relationship with a Muslim unless he had a foundation in apologetics and if he was deep in his Christian faith." For Eman, Islam was an essential part of who she was: it was how she dressed, how she connected; it shaped her way of existing in the world. She shares, "For Muslim people, Islam means family, means unity, means *umma*, you know, nation. Islam is not only a religion, it is an identity, a whole identity, a whole history; our roots, our ancestors." All of that changed when she first questioned her belief in Islam, and then found faith in Jesus. However, her surrender to Christ was the beginning of a lifelong struggle.

Fast-forward several years and both are enrolled as seminary students at the ABTS in Beirut, taking courses on Islam developed by IMES. Interestingly, they both had similar initial reactions to IMES's approach of dialoguing with, and even developing close personal relationships with, Muslims. "I was surprised by the school of thought that Martin was using and that he lives out, which was coexistence with Muslims – living together in peace with Muslims in society and having a relationship with them," admits George. "I thought, 'Yes, I think this approach could work in Lebanon, but it would fail in Egypt.' That was my thought during the first year."

While George was initially incredulous but cautiously accepting, Eman dismissed the entire concept as absurd. "I remember when I heard the vision for the first time. I felt that this is hilarious, because you will never find a way to communicate with Muslims without compromising Christianity, because Muslims want us to confess the Qur'an; that the Bible is not correct, and our faith is not correct. That is how they respond every time when we start a conversation."

For both students, their change in perceptions was gradual, but deeply significant.

George is now so convinced of the IMES approach that he plans at some point to pursue a degree in Muslim-Christian relations. He is now back in Egypt, promoting this concept of interfaith dialogue and peaceful coexistence as part of his church ministry. It is clear how passionate he has become about this vision of transforming society through the promotion of genuine, mutual understanding. George's underlying assumption, like IMES's vision, is a theology of active engagement for the benefit of society. "This is very important for justice in our society, that I and the Muslim are against darkness, against taking advantage of the other, and against corruption. This is a vision bigger than just talking about religion." He clearly links this to fulfilling the church's calling to incarnate Christ to the world around us, putting him on display in both word and deed. He describes how, when Christians live this out properly in front of their Muslim neighbours, they can dispel misconceptions and incorrect notions of what it truly means to be a follower of Christ. One implication is that this can only be successful when we embrace the Muslim "other" and fight together against injustice, inequality and oppression.

As a "Muslim background follower of Jesus," Eman's journey has been more complex. Her initial vehement response to IMES's approach was perhaps related to her own conversion process and the response of the Christian church in Egypt. She recounts, somewhat painfully, how churches in Egypt often encourage new converts to sever all ties with their families and Muslim communities, without offering them in return the kind of relational and emotional support they so desperately need. "It is like taking a fish from the sea and putting it in the air or on the ground," she explains mournfully, "so it will die. And that is what we feel like when we leave our families; when we leave our Muslim communities." She further describes this experience in poignant terms: "It is very hard to leave a place you belong to, with all your memories, leave everyone you loved. Something inside you feels that you are not loving them anymore, you feel like you no longer know them, and maybe you feel that they are your enemy; this is very hard. The church must understand this truth about the converted, that they are suffering a lot, and they have this struggle with themselves and with their past. They start to hate themselves, they start to hate their history, they start to hate everything they love. This is not Christian."

By the time Eman arrived at ABTS she had learned to assimilate herself to Christian culture to the extent that she too hated Muslims, and with them, a part of herself. Though resistant at first, it was eventually through the work of IMES that she was able to work through these feelings of animosity. She explains how IMES starts by reconciling people, particularly Muslim-background believers, to themselves. "Later on, I understood. Martin was instrumental in me starting to call my family again. I realized that I do not belong to that place anymore. However, I feel better when I have this kind of relationship with my family because they are still my family. I owe them everything in my life. Christianity is not to leave your family or to not do your duties in your family. You have to be committed with your family, because this is the teaching of Jesus. To do the right thing; to be the light and salt."

Eman and her husband now lead a fruitful ministry among Muslim followers of Jesus in Lebanon, and she is slowly working towards a place of healing and restoration with her family back in Egypt. When she and her husband graduate from the seminary, she dreams of permanently returning to Egypt and working to build up the local church with an emphasis on learning from the experiences of Muslim background followers. "For the Arab church it is very important because we have a new generation of believers from a Muslim background who feel like mutants in the church. We need to understand Islam more, to understand the behaviour of followers from non-Christian backgrounds and their feelings, what the changes are in their lives, how they have to deal with it, to feel with them, to respect what they believe in." She believes that this mission is imperative as such believers will soon shape and transform the future of the church in Egypt, and across the region.

A Tale of Two Communities: Pre-emptive Ministry and a Catalyst for Peace-Making

Israel's brief but devastating 2006 offensive against Hezbollah's strongholds in southern and eastern parts of Lebanon left over a million people internally displaced (see appendix). In an act of unexpected compassion, ABTS contacted some of the Shi'ite clerics and religious leaders with whom IMES had built relationships and whose communities had borne the brunt of the bombing to ask how they were coping. Their honest answer was that they were not. In response, ABTS, and its affiliate the Beirut Baptist School, opened their doors to host over a thousand displaced families providing them with shelter, food and clothing.

Looking back at this experience, Martin Accad remarked, "I think we need to think about mission more as preparing for what God is doing and about to do. It is about being pre-emptive. What is the point of building a network of relationships with Muslims? In times of crisis or in a situation where conflict could have emerged, there are relationships that can actually be used at the service of peace and peace-making." Many at ABTS and throughout the Lebanese Society for Educational and Social Development (LSESD) now reference the 2006 relief response as perhaps the quintessential example of such peace-making work. For many in the Christian community, it was their first meaningful contact with Muslims since the Lebanese Civil War. "We made a conscious decision at that time not to preach, just to serve," reports Development and Partner Relations director of the LSESD, Alia Abboud. This event led to the establishment of the *Relief and Community Development* division of the organization. This ministry now serves thousands of refugees and internally displaced people across the region, irrespective of religion or creed.

motivation – the love of Christ not simply doing good.

This is not the only ministry that developed as a result of this single instance of reaching out across sectarian lines. "Initiatives that some of my colleagues here at ABTS or people in our circles started among displaced Shi'ites have endured to this day," continues Accad. "There is a particular ministry among women that started in 2006 that is still ongoing. People would not even have thought that they should or could do anything like that if they had not already been transformed in their thinking about who Muslims are and the possibilities of relating to them."

IMES's work has sometimes been mis-characterized as merely dialogue with no real component of Christian witness. However, IMES attempts to maintain the two goals of dialogue and witness in parallel, not one at the expense of the other. Accad reflects on the importance of finding this balance if we are to pursue loving relationships with Muslims on the basis of mutual understanding. "It is easier to keep Muslims at arm's length if you just want to use an aggressive evangelistic approach," he explains,

> because the moment you start seeing them as people that you can actually talk to, then, "Maybe I need to re-think my polemics?" Also, if you re-think your polemics, does that mean you give up on evangelism? Yet it does not feel right just to build friendships. What we are trying to do is walk this very thin line, where we want to really explore how can you maintain both? How can you have a missional approach to dialogue, and how can you have a dialogical approach to witnessing about Jesus to individual Muslims and to Muslims as a community?

While IMES has emerged as a leading voice in the global evangelical conversation on interfaith relations, as well as on the role and future of Christianity in the Middle East, its proponents still prefer to keep their work closer to home. Here the soil may be rockier, but this is the land where they feel called to sow their seeds of peace and reconciliation; seeds of the gospel that may soon find themselves in a fertile field, and that field may soon grow into a forest.

Missiological Reflection: Witness Requires Dialogue and Dialogue Requires Witness (by Martin Accad)

The three tales recounted above all reflect a development in the attitude and approach of the two theologians, students and communities. They all begin with suspicious attitudes derived from negative experiences in their backgrounds, yet gradually move towards greater trust and love, which result from personal encounter and friendship. The suspicion, often verging on hatred, is the natural propensity of individuals and communities with a history of conflict and hurt. The memories of war, persecution and suffering have driven Christians and Muslims apart, and their communities have remained separated by firm, yet invisible, boundaries for the greater part of their histories.

In 2004, shortly after beginning to engage in interaction with Muslims through the IMES, I quickly realized the extent to which the concept of dialogue was misunderstood within my evangelical community. Dialogue was a dirty word which was immediately associated with compromise and "selling out." In other circles, where evangelicals had a solid reputation for "sheep-stealing," IMES's dialogue initiatives were seen as little more than disguised efforts at proselytism. With a genuine desire for greater rapprochement and respectful understanding, yet with a deep concern for the preservation of the evangelical distinctive of mission and witness to the saving grace of God in Christ, I began to explore other possibilities for genuine engagement on the spectrum between the extremes of syncretism and polemics. This effort led to the emergence of IMES's unique approach to "dialogical witness," which I have dubbed *Kerygmatic* interaction. This was eventually better documented in my chapter entitled "Christian Attitudes toward Islam and Muslims: A *Kerygmatic* Approach," published in 2012 as part of *Essays in Honor of J. Dudley Woodberry*.[25]

The *Kerygmatic* approach seeks to emulate God's model, who engaged us historically by coming to us in Christ and interacting with us in a witness of love and self-giving that led to death by crucifixion. As he continues to encounter us by living with us and in us through his Holy Spirit, he draws us out and away from the safety of our exclusivist communities and church walls, and invites us to encounter in the same way those whom social conventions would have us view as enemies. The *Kerygmatic* approach believes that there is no faithful witness without dialogue, and no authentic dialogue without witness. It is the incarnational approach which God modelled for us.

All three tales recounted in the case study document a movement on the spectrum of Christian-Muslim interaction, with two theologians, two students and two communities irresistibly drawn towards the *kerygmatic*. The two theologians, both involved regularly in the existential kind of "dialogue of life" find themselves engaged in theological conversations about commonalities

---

25. Evelyne A. Reisacher, ed., *Toward Respectful Understanding and Witness among Muslims* (Pasadena: William Carey Library, 2012), 29–47. See also Andrews, *Church in Disorienting Times*, 94–96 and 117–120.

and differences, often controversial and thorny, as a result of intense interaction and life together. The two students, George and Eman, despite their vastly different backgrounds, had come to the deadlocks of polemics and apologetics as a result of historical wounds and personal hurt. The one had retreated into Christian isolationism, while the other had been driven to social separation from her community of birth. The possibility of reconciliation offered to them by the IMES ethos led them both back to a place of deep and mature personal relationship with their mixed communities and families. It is hard to overstate the pain that the church inflicts on members who have joined the *body* from non-Christian backgrounds when they push them to cut themselves off from their communities of birth. The disciples of Jesus were not "called out" (literal meaning of "church," from *ekklesia* in Greek) to form exclusivist communities in the margins of society. What we find Jesus doing, on the contrary, is inviting individuals who have been marginalized by the social mainstream, calling them into the divine mainstream. Christ's *ekklesia* is expected to be salt and light *in* the world, not to remove itself *out of* the world. "Go home + tell them ... begin

The IMES approach encourages followers of Jesus from Muslim backgrounds to maintain a vibrant presence and witness in their contexts, among their family and immediate community. While other approaches, such as the apologetic defence of the faith, or the more aggressive approach of polemics, may bear fruit in the short term, the dialogical approach to mission bears better fruit in the longer term. The first two cause persons to be rejected by their society so that they become outsiders, whereas the *kerygmatic* approach leads to mature persons who are able to remain in society and maintain their identity in the Arab world. They can continue to live in their contexts and do not have to leave and go elsewhere. Islam is a diverse religious phenomenon with a multiplicity of manifestations. There is, in fact, much to embrace and learn from the faith of Muslim people all over the world. While one might easily point to that which is distorted and grotesque, one might equally discover that which is admirable and worthy of emulation.

As for the two communities that had been living each in their sectarian ghetto, the *kerygmatic* attitude which had gradually become part of the culture of the small Baptist community around ABTS kicked them into Christ-like action, triggered by a sudden intense crisis. The *kerygmatic*, dialogical kind of mission carries the significant benefit of being not only proactive in its peacebuilding, but also pre-emptive in volatile contexts that can easily drift into conflict and war. A number of people over the years have asked me why should IMES be established within ABTS: was this not going to restrict its vision? But the point is that we do not exist for ourselves. We exist to provoke change. We want to be catalysts for change within the community where we belong, even when it is not easy. The driving impetus behind the founding of IMES was not merely to provide new insight into Muslim-Christian relations, but to re-think what it means for the church in the Middle East, and specifically for the Protestant and evangelical church, to be missional in a Muslim context and to be witnesses to Jesus in this region.

At the global level, the events of 11 September 2001 (9–11) marked the beginning of an intense conflict between East and West, Christians and Muslims, in dramatic fulfilment of Samuel Huntington's ominous thesis of a "clash of civilizations."[26] By 2008, Muslims and Christians had come to realize that the future of the planet was largely going to depend on their ability to coexist peacefully. In a letter endorsed initially by 138 Muslim scholars from around the world (and eventually signed by hundreds more), the *Royal Aal al Bayt Institute* of Amman, Jordan, initiated an invitation to Christians everywhere to come to "A Common Word" with Muslims, inspired by the Qur'an's third chapter, *Al-'Imran*, verse 64. The first paragraph of the letter reads:

> Muslims and Christians together make up well over half of the world's population. Without peace and justice between these two religious communities, there can be no meaningful peace in the world. The future of the world depends on peace between Muslims and Christians.[27]

This was a remarkable initiative. But it was the Yale response to "A Common Word," published within a month of the Muslim initiative, which precipitated the evangelical world into the untested waters of *evangelical* dialogue with Islam.[28] Until then, the global Protestant world had been divided into two broad camps: mainline Protestants who had a venerable history of dialogue with Islam, and evangelical Protestants who had so far contented themselves with the mission of the evangelization of Muslims. The initiation of a gracious dialogical response by respected evangelical theologian Miroslav Volf, and other evangelical colleagues at the *Yale Center for Faith and Culture*, opened up new horizons for the more conservative Protestant traditions.

Be that as it may, the idea of a "dialogical witness" is still by no means unanimously accepted in the conservative evangelical world, which is

---

26. Samuel Huntington, *The Clash of Civilizations and the Remaking of World Order* (New York: Touchstone, 1996).

27. http://www.acommonword.com/the-acw-document/ (accessed 3 September 2016).

28. http://faith.yale.edu/common-word/common-word-christian-response (accessed 3 September 2016).

still rattled by the 2008 developments. Numerous efforts, organizations, programmes and initiatives of dialogue have been launched by evangelicals since then, and with these, as many reactionary counter-efforts continue to split that community globally like birth-pangs. Evangelical theologians still have a long way to go in developing a proper biblical theology of Islam that fits their conservative worldview in a consistent manner. Much creative work, research and writing has yet to be done, particularly in the field of soteriology (see glossary), to develop a mature synthesis between dialogue and witness in the mission enterprise. But the river has broken open and there is no backtracking: the evangelical church of the Middle East stands both as pioneer, trailblazer and partner in this exciting journey as part of the mission of God.

7

Peacebuilding in the Mission of God

Our journey through spheres of missional engagement moves smoothly from dialogue to the related topic of peacebuilding. As Christians, we follow the God of peace. How do we express that, and how can our engagement with society include being peacemakers? We have noted that there is conflict in many parts of the MENA region. We look at conflict at both large scale and also more intimately amongst individuals and within local communities.

The background material addresses the critique that religion is the cause of much of the conflict seen in the world. Our first two case studies are from Egypt, describing the work of two Christian leaders bringing peace to individuals and, wherever possible, communities. The third case study describes the work of Musalaha in seeking to bring peace amongst Jewish and Palestinian peoples starting from individuals of both ethnicities. This organisation was founded and is led by Salim Munayer.

In several places in this chapter it is noted that the work of peacebuilding requires dialogue amongst Muslims, Christians and others. Our focus here builds on the previous chapter. Our deliberations are provided by Salim Munayer together with Jesse Wheeler (see contributors' bios) and Samah Fakhreldein.

Background: What Does Religion Have to Do with Peace? (by Jesse Wheeler)

Religion is often regarded as a primary cause of regional and global conflict, and those raging in the Middle East today are cited as examples supporting that view.[1] Conflicts in places like Iraq, Syria, Lebanon, Yemen, Israel/Palestine, Sudan and Egypt are full of contentious religious fault lines featuring sectarian militias, religious radicalism, apocalyptic millenarianism, and ethnic – or, more accurately, confessional – cleansing.

Traditionally, Western thought has seen a secularized public sphere as the best way to curb conflict. This instinct was forged in the chaos of the confessional-driven Thirty Years' War and developed further in Enlightenment-based reasoning. These historical ideas are now nearly axiomatic,[2] even within parts of the church, and have dramatically shaped the manner by which peace-making is undertaken worldwide.[3] What does religion have to do with peace? Many would argue: not much and nothing good. One's deepest held beliefs, the richest vein of identity, are too threatening to political order.

Yet the prevailing scepticism about religion in public life gives too much credit to religious belief as an inevitable source of conflict and ignores its potential role as a true catalyst for peace. "Rarely is conflict between two religious groups simply a matter of theological difference or religious misunderstanding,"[4] and this is as true for the conflicts of the MENA region as it is for other conflict zones around the world. The popular notion that the Israeli-Palestinian conflict is simply the continuation of a millennia-long struggle between the children of Abraham fundamentally ignores key drivers of a late modern conflict.[5] To describe the "new cold war" between Saudi Arabia and Iran as simply another episode in the centuries long Sunni-Shi'a

---

1. Abu-Nimer, Khoury, and Welty, *Unity in Diversity*, 7.

2. Axiomatic, namely, taken as true because it is presumed to be self-evident.

3. See Nancey Murphy, *Beyond Liberalism and Fundamentalism: How Modern and Postmodern Philosophy Set the Theological Agenda* (New York: Trinity Press International, 2007).

4. Abu-Nimer, Khoury, and Welty, *Unity in Diversity*, 21.

5. Many great, as well as troublesome, histories exist of the Israeli-Palestinian conflict. However, I would be remiss not to recommend Colin Chapman's *Whose Promised Land?: The Continuing Crisis over Israel and Palestine* (Oxford: Lion Hudson, 2015). Chapman has served as Lead Faculty for MENA Islam in IMES's Master of Religion in Middle Eastern and North African Studies programme.

divide would be to glibly dismiss the legitimate political-economic factors and socio-cultural dynamics currently at work in that relationship.[6]

But traditional diplomatic peace-making efforts – approaches that do not address the religious narratives of a conflict, or engage the religious communities caught within a conflict – have largely proven ineffective. One can legitimately challenge the authenticity of the motives of the various actors involved in the diplomatic process, but to say that religion has no role to play in perpetuating conflict would also be problematic. Referring to the Israel-Palestine peace process, Muhammad Abu-Nimer, Amal Khoury and Emily Welty write:

> There is an apparent secularization of the peace process. The religious aspects of the process – Jewish, Christian, Muslim – have been ignored by politicians and decision makers in all formal and informal negotiations. By failing to integrate the religious dimensions of the conflict, these political agreements and processes have alienated significant segments of both Palestinian and Israeli societies.[7]

A viable peace process must account for the socio-political makeup of Middle Eastern society and the central role religion plays within that society in transmitting historical narratives, shaping worldviews, motivating behaviours and defining the relationship between individuals and the communities to which they belong, including religious ones. Yet, these have been largely ignored, as Marc Gopin observes:

> The role of religion in perpetuating the principal conflict hardly needs delineation. But even more lies below the surface, much more that needs to be exposed. It is essential, therefore, as an outgrowth of such analysis, to integrate the relevant cultural values of these people into a deepened peace-making process. This has not been attempted until now by most scholars of conflict, conflict resolution activists, or diplomats, and as a result the peace process has barely penetrated the moral consciousness of either side.[8]

---

6. Numerous sources have begun in recent years to speak of a "Cold War" between Saudi Arabia and Iran. For example: Curtis Ryan, "The New Arab Cold War and the Struggle for Syria," *Middle East Report* 262 (Spring 2012).

7. Abu-Nimer, Khoury, and Welty, *Unity in Diversity*, 45.

8. Marc Gopin, *Holy War, Holy Peace: How Religion Can Bring Peace to the Middle East* (New York: Oxford University Press, 2002), 6.

Although it may not be the primary cause for any specific conflict, religion can decisively shape the course of a conflict, although in different ways than initially thought.

For a variety of historical and sociological factors, the concept of "identity" in Middle Eastern cultures is profoundly religious. According to missiologist Jens Barnett:

> Identity is closely related to narrative thinking. My identity – including all my relationships – is constructed in the present as I selectively recollect and appropriate experiences from my past. Not only does this narrated montage of memories tell me who I am and who is important to me, but by stringing these events together to form a coherent story, it also fills my life with meaning and purpose.
>
> This sense of purpose shapes my values, goals and future choices. By projecting my story forward into the future, I know what I should do next. As I stay true to this idealistic narrative, my decisions grow into habits, and eventually take on a permanence that I and others begin to recognize as typically "me."[9]

More often than not, identity – that is, one's sense of self, purpose and meaning – is embedded within a deeply religious narrative and embodied by a specific faith community attached to a particular location. Simply put, identity naturally encompasses the political. In Lebanon, for example, topographical segregation and a confessional-based education system have resulted in the absence of a singular "national unifying collective memory. Each community has its own, which inhibits the creation of one common history,"[10] and therefore also the formation of a broader or shared cross-confessional identity. In Egypt, too, researchers "often found competing narratives about the reality of life in Egypt today"[11] and "it became clear . . . that sectarian feelings predominate and supersede those of national unity."[12] Even in Jordan, "while Christians as a group were not singled out as 'other' . . . the fact that the majority of the Christian population in Jordan happens to be Palestinian seems to be of consequence."[13]

---

9. Jens Barnett, "Narrative, Identity and Discipleship," *Musafir: A Bulletin of Intercultural Studies* 3, no. 2 (December 2009): 3–5.

10. Abu-Nimer, Khoury, and Welty, *Unity in Diversity*, 101.

11. Abu-Nimer, Khoury, Welty, 141.

12. Abu-Nimer, Khoury, Welty, 148.

13. Abu-Nimer, Khoury, Welty, 181.

As a result, the MENA region often witnesses conflict between identities and worldviews, not just between individuals and communities. In the words of Abu-Nimer, Khoury and Welty:

> The Middle East . . . is deeply affected by religious identities and meanings, and its conflicts require reconciliation processes that recognize that religiousness. A comprehensive peace based solely on secular values, actors and frameworks will not be sustainable; peace must involve the religious believers and resonate with their faith.[14]

The central place of religion in the MENA region does contribute to the perpetuation of a conflict, and so it is also critical to its resolution.[15] But to promote peace by means of secularization is, in many ways, to directly challenge the very identity and worldview of those engaged in conflict, with the very real possibility of doing more harm than good.

Protestant missionaries to the Middle East in the nineteenth and twentieth centuries quickly encountered this inescapable socio-political reality. Rev Dr Habib Badr describes Middle Eastern society as one "where confessions and confessionalism play a basic role in people's daily lives; it was not possible for a person to change his or her own personal conviction in such a way that left his [sic] family, social, economic and political life untouched."[16] As a result, political engagement became a necessity for Protestant missionaries and churches from the start. That reality is true today for Christians in the region. We cannot simply avoid political questions in our Christian witness to the world. Rather, we must reason and act in accordance with our faith.

Many questions emerge, then, about the task of peace-making and political engagement in the mission of God. How do we imagine and might possibly re-imagine religion's role in conflict? In what ways does our own faith and community of belonging shape how we understand current conflicts today? How can religious commitments contribute to peacebuilding, and what prevents those contributions from happening? What does religion – my own, my neighbour's – have to do with peace, a peace that my neighbour and I must inhabit and share? What if my neighbour is my enemy?

Moreover, what can and should evangelical Christians in the MENA countries contribute to the political life of their respective countries? What

---

14. Abu-Nimer, Khoury, Welty, 9–10.

15. Gopin, *Holy War, Holy Peace*, 7–8.

16. Badr, "Evangelical Churches," 714.

do Christians believe about the nature and purpose of political power in light of the kingdom of God?

Case Studies: Servants of Peace: Three Stories (by Samah Fakhreldein)

Our three case studies explore these questions. The first two are from Egypt and the third is based in Jerusalem.

A Development Practitioner Seeks Peace

"I serve humans for the sake of our common humanity, regardless of their religious background." These words of Dr Andrea Zaki, General Director of the Coptic Evangelical Organization for Social Services in Egypt (CEOSS), describe what motivates and permeates his ministry with the poor and marginalized during conflict.

When asked why he chose to serve God through peacebuilding, using a community development approach, Zaki responded by giving three examples of transformed lives of individuals.

> I have seen a very poor widow with five children who had lost her means of subsistence and was neglected, ignorant and devoid of hope, have her dignity restored as a result of a small project she created after receiving support from CEOSS. I have witnessed an illiterate father learn how to read and write and as a result be restored to a place of respect in society. I have observed two village leaders, one Muslim and the other Christian, who used to hate each other join together in an interfaith forum, reconcile and develop a friendship based on mutual respect and subsequently open an institute teaching the children of the village how to coexist. Examples such as these are why I choose this approach to serve God's kingdom.

Zaki's family was Christian but not evangelical. At the age of sixteen his friend invited him to a youth meeting during which he decided to give his life to Jesus. He joined an evangelical church and dedicated his life to ministry. He had a growing conviction to serve the kingdom of God by building peace in times of conflict. During the early years of his theological studies, Zaki felt called to minister among the marginalized and the poor. A professor asked him to write about his vision for ministry and then urged Zaki to retain the resulting paper and re-read it twenty years hence. Zaki did so, noting that his vision remained the same: "serving humans for the sake of our common humanity, regardless of religious background, serving the poor and the marginalized, and witnessing a spiritual and cultural transformation in society."

After receiving his bachelor's degree, Zaki was ordained in 1987 as a development pastor in CEOSS. After furthering his education in social development in Canada and theology in the United States, focusing on social change, he continued on to complete a PhD in religion and theology, his studies charting a pioneering course. "I feel I was chosen for this as part of God's plan for my life."

As a regional expert in political religion and the theological foundations for social change, Zaki became the general director of CEOSS in 2010. He describes CEOSS as one of the largest NGOs in the Middle East, serving almost two million marginalized Egyptians through its development projects annually and almost one million through the *Forum of Intercultural Dialogue*. This forum deals with political and economic issues facing Egypt and engages Christian and Muslim leaders, as well as government officials and intellectuals, in face-to-face dialogue.[17] Zaki is committed to serving the kingdom by using all the gifts and skills available at CEOSS to bring about peace and justice in society.

A Pastoral Approach to Building Bridges

"I am a pastor of Muslims too!" What prompted Rev Radi Atallah, pastor of the Attarein Presbyterian Church in Alexandria, Egypt, to utter these words?

A Muslim was killed in a tragic work-related accident, and no one in the community was willing to help the man's family remove his body from the hospital. That was until some people from the neighbourhood approached Rev Atallah, who overcame his initial hesitation and provided practical support. A local official was surprised, asking, "You are a Christian pastor and the dead guy is Muslim, so why do you help him?" Radi's reply was emphatic: "I am a pastor of Muslims too!"

Rev Atallah is the president of the Council of Ministry and Development in his synod, serving six hundred churches, and he leads four NGOs that serve society through a variety of community development and peacebuilding initiatives. He has a passion for the poor and marginalized in his society. "I felt the need for reconciliation in our societies; our society is torn apart. We do

---

17. See http://en.ceoss-eg.org/about-us/who-we-are-2/ (accessed 20 April 2018).

not accept one another. We are blind with the anger and fear we have inherited over the course of history."

Although there has never been a civil war between Muslims and Christians in Egypt, there is a long history of hatred and sectarianism between the two communities. The city of Alexandria is known for having a particularly bloody history of sectarian tension. Rev Atallah started the initiative "Building Bridges" during a period of attacks and counter attacks from both sides of the confessional divide. There seemed to be an absence of collective wisdom, which prompted Rev Atallah to contact fellow political and religious leaders in the area. Building Bridges consists of an interfaith forum between Christian and Muslims leaders in Alexandria and bridge building activities amongst youth in the universities. In addition, Rev Atallah recently began a youth initiative focused on sports whereby Christians and Muslims play together in religiously mixed teams. In reference to this, he commented, "We spent years in meetings on so-called interfaith-dialogue, but there has been no real change in society. So, I started a new interfaith dialogue group wherein the youth lead, and community leaders bless."

Rev Atallah's peacebuilding initiatives have resulted in his being more engaged with political life in Egypt, as these denominational conflicts directly affect the political situation of the country. When asked about his political activities, he responded:

> my role as a Christian is not only to respect the political authority, but also to stand against injustice and use my voice as an Egyptian citizen. One year during Ramadan, two youths from my church were arrested on the charge of "disrespecting religion." Two teenagers from poor families were distributing a message from the sermon on the mountain about love. It was not a crime, but the government saw it as a crime. In response, we as a church stood beside these kids and their families, using our collective political voice in their defence. We have to use the voice of wisdom and reason in our lives as Christians.

As the head of his church, Rev Atallah began building bridges of peace in his society through friendships and dialogue motivated by love, believing this spirit would spread throughout both Christian and Muslim communities. He still believes in the power of peace and its centrality to the kingdom of God.

Musalaha: A Ministry of Reconciliation

"We yearned to see followers of Jesus unite around their common faith as an example to the rest of society, showing tangible evidence of Christ's love and light through their reconciled relationships as Palestinians and Israelis," the words of Dr Salim Munayer, co-founder and leader of Musalaha (Arabic for reconciliation),[18] a non-profit organization that promotes and facilitates reconciliation between Israelis and Palestinians from diverse ethnic and religious backgrounds based on the life and teaching of Jesus.

As a Palestinian-Israeli born to a family of six children, Munayer wrote his doctoral study on "The Ethnic Identity of Palestinian Arab Christian Adolescents in Israel" informed by his own life story. Munayer founded Musalaha in 1990 with Pastor Evan Thomas, a Messianic Jewish friend (see glossary) and congregation leader, along with other Palestinian Christian and Messianic Jewish leaders, as "a response to the division that became apparent in society and the church during the First Intifada of the Israeli-Palestinian conflict" (see appendix).

Munayer and his team recognized the need for Musalaha as they felt in their everyday lives that their respective communities, Palestinian Christian and Messianic Jewish Israeli, were divided along theological, ideological, and nationalistic lines. Believers in the same Lord saw each other as enemies. So, the work of Musalaha has focused on Palestinian and Israeli societies, working among opinion shapers within their communities. They also recognized the critical role of women and youth in peace and reconciliation movements and began working with both to develop leaders with skills for peacebuilding.

The Arab church is served by Musalaha also, especially on the issue of unity and reconciliation within the local body of Christ, "as our testimony to the outside world comes from who we are together, as followers of Jesus. It addresses the major need of the community for reconciliation amidst our many conflicts. And, it provides a prophetic voice in society, speaking candidly about issues of peace and justice as informed by God's kingdom." Musalaha has opened doors within the larger society as a testimony to who Jesus is. "When we do reconciliation, people ask us about Jesus. Through this work, segments of Jewish and Muslim societies are open to engage with Christians when they would otherwise not be, especially in regard to the issues we all face in society as a whole."

---

18. www.musalaha.org/ (accessed 11 December 2018).

Musalaha also provides space for Palestinian Christians to reach across many barriers to know, come to love, and practise forgiveness with their Israeli sisters and brothers in Christ. It makes it possible for members of the Arab Church in Palestine, and for those located within the State of Israel, to practically live out forgiveness of their enemies and release the bitterness that comes with living under occupation or as second-class citizens.

In addition, Musalaha provides training in leadership and reconciliation for members of the church. Musalaha's *Curriculum of Reconciliation* takes participants through a two-year period of relationship building and working through the stages of reconciliation, going beyond the superficial "Hallelujah and hummus" phase of intercommunal interaction to a place of deep introspection, self-reflection and, eventually, collective action. Importantly, the approach takes seriously the more group and family-oriented nature of Middle Eastern culture. Musalaha's methodology has been shaped in response to the specific obstacles to reconciliation that are unique to the Israeli-Palestinian conflict and context, among Muslims, Jews and Christians, but the insights have been applied elsewhere.

Grass-roots work is key to peacebuilding in society, Munayer believes, and reconciliation work at this level is far more powerful in creating a lasting peace between communities. He also believes that the church cannot simply avoid political questions. Domestic and foreign political realities, including the threat of fear, intimidation and violence, can prevent grassroots movements from forming within civil society. Foreign involvement, whether political, economic or religious intervention from Arab extremist groups or Western radical millenarian groups (see glossary), often amplifies already existing obstacles towards reconciliation.

Musalaha has introduced an alternative narrative in conflict infested with hatred and enmity. The community of people who have responded to this new approach have found a different way to relate to the conflict, one that is starkly different to that found within much of Israeli and Palestinian society. Munayer dreams of a community of people who say, "We want to live life differently. We are not willing to compromise the gospel and its teachings."

Concluding Reflection

A distinct pattern emerges from the stories of these three leaders that reflects how God empowers all of his people in the work of his kingdom. First, each had a living encounter with the reconciling God. God reached out in reconciliation to them, personally, in Jesus, and extended the blessings of his globe-spanning kingdom to them. As a result of this encounter, Zaki, Atallah, and Munayer now give witness to the reality of the kingdom of God and are empowered for ministry. But, importantly, their calls led them into ministry beyond their own community of belonging. They do not see their role as leaders as primarily to benefit their own community. Instead, each works to reach beyond and across these old, familiar boundaries of identification and conflict. They see peace-making and political engagement – especially that which is done on behalf of their neighbours of a different faith – as part of their work in God's kingdom. This pattern is normative to a kingdom approach to peace and political engagement.

Missiological Reflection: Living as Citizens of the Kingdom of God (by Salim Munayer)

For Christians the foundation of reconciliation – indeed, the hope of any reconciliation – is the kingdom of God. Mere method and technique do not advance lasting peacebuilding work. Rather, reconciliation efforts must be deeply rooted in the reality of God's kingdom, the here-and-not-yet eschatological reality begun by God in Christ. As Christians, we follow and imitate God's own reconciling lead into places of conflict, suffering and injustice: we pray for and seek to make peace with our enemies, and we do so because God has done that with us, we who were once *his* enemies. The works of reconciliation are carried out in faithful witness to the work of God in Christ who is reconciling the world to himself and who has made us ambassadors for Christ, making his appeal through us in the ministry of reconciliation (2 Cor 5:18–21).

There are many faith-based approaches that one could take in peacebuilding and reconciliation. Some have real merit. However, too many of them focus narrowly on individual reconciliation and are tailored to a Western cultural outlook, neglecting the larger group and family aspects of identity prevalent in the MENA region (and other non-Western contexts). Many lack even a rudimentary understanding of Middle Eastern cultures. Other approaches are far too clinical or merely sociological, using only selective passages from the Bible to discern abstract principles from case studies of key characters. Again, while these approaches may offer some valuable insights, they are limited in addressing larger communal and ethnic divisions.

Another popular peace-making approach emphasizes the role of intercession, a spiritual discipline we strongly affirm. But the approach has serious problematic elements, not least of which are the ways it conflates ancient Israel with nations today and its understanding of repentance.[19] While "identificational repentance" (see glossary) is not an idea altogether absent in Scripture, the concept as it is popularly taught today downplays the importance of wrong-doers making their own confession of repentance to God. Prayer and repentance are fundamental in a kingdom approach to peace-making, but when Jesus announced the kingdom of God, he called people to repentance, not to "identificational repentance" (Matt 4:17).

A kingdom approach to peacebuilding entails both vertical and horizontal reconciliation: God pursues reconciliation with people (vertical) and thereby makes it possible for people to be reconciled with one another (horizontal). "The vertical and horizontal aspects of reconciliation are interdependent and mutually reinforcing, and bear witness to one another. True 'horizontal reconciliation' is dependent on prior 'vertical reconciliation.'"[20]

The reality of God's kingdom spans history, beginning with the biblical account of the people of Israel and finding its fulfilment in Jesus Christ. Indeed, the narrative of Israel is inextricably connected to how we understand Jesus's pronunciation of the kingdom of God. But the idea of God's kingdom underwent transformations in the life of Israel, especially during the Babylonian exile. In Christ, we see that the good news of the kingdom encompasses the whole earth. Peacebuilding work that is grounded in the kingdom of God flows from this biblical and historical stream.

What is the kingdom of God like? It is a kingdom that is *for* the world, not *from* it. It does not obey the logic of worldly kingdoms. It is not established nor maintained by violent force, as most temporal rule is, using raw power to establish legitimacy. Rather, Jesus's arrival and kingdom inauguration were marked by a lack of violence and coercion. At the same time, not insignificantly, the Scriptures remark at his unique authority made manifest in his teachings (Matt 7:28–29) and miracles, with his legitimate power over disease, dark spiritual forms, and the chaos of nature. But even in his manifest authority, Jesus's kingship is marked by service and self-giving (Mark 10:45). Those who

---

19. See, for example, the teaching of John Dawson on "identificational repentance," especially in his books *What Christians Should Know about Reconciliation* (first published 1998) and *Healing America's Wounds* (Delight: Gospel Light Publications, 1994). David Damien, a popular conference convener with a substantial following of Chinese Christians, includes symbolic performances of identificational repentance in his events. Examples include Egyptian women performing a kind of "repentance ceremony" on behalf of Hagar to a representational Sarah, and a "symbolic marriage ceremony" performed between two people representing the Jews and the Arabs.

20. Salim J. Munayer and Lisa Loden, *Through My Enemies' Eyes: Envisioning Reconciliation in Israel-Palestine* (Milton Keynes: Paternoster, 2013), 192.

follow this Servant-King imitate that life of service and self-giving. It is a kingdom that does not obliterate the world with its authority, but pursues, redeems and reconciles with it.

The kingdom of God also upends the predictable forms of superiority and social institutions that are established in violence, power, fame and fortune. As Mary announced in the Magnificat (Luke 1:46–55), the kingdom of God relativizes all that this world lifts up as important and life-giving. Moreover, conflicts at all levels are resolved in the kingdom of God. Long-standing lines of division along ethnic identity or social standing are transformed, bringing those from different backgrounds into actual relationship, where all are mutually benefitted. In the kingdom of God, no difference is greater than he who unites us.

This cross-centred unity implies that our citizenship in the kingdom of God informs our identity and judges whatever idolatrous identification we have with "our tribe" and "our nation." In the kingdom of God, believers are offered new identities, having become new creations, and are now called "citizens." We are not merely passive subjects of personal salvation. As citizens, we are empowered by the Holy Spirit to work as ambassadors in the ministry of reconciliation. With our new identity secured as representatives of this kingdom, we are called to go beyond the limits of the believing community and proclaim the good news of the kingdom to all individuals, to all nations, so they too might become citizens of the kingdom.

In obedience to the King who is above all rulers, believers have an obligation to proclaim the nearness and reality of this kingdom to all, even to the reigning temporal powers. The modern nation-state cannot and does not define the meaning of life, which it constantly arrogates to itself in ignorance, deception and corruption. It is the responsibility of the community of believers, whatever the cost may be, to remind the rulers of their task of governance – which is limited, passing and operates always under the judgment of the King of kings – and to call them to account. In prayer and political engagement, Christians must contribute to the common good of all, out of obedience to our Lord expressed in love for our neighbours. Insofar as the church needs a theology of reconciliation, which speaks of the possibility of peace for our conflicts today, we also need to articulate a political theology for how to engage with those who rule, which speaks to the possibility of meaningful, cruciform political engagement.

There are good reasons to be sceptical and wary about Christian political engagement. The sordid history of Middle Eastern Christians' close alignment with Arab nationalism and its strong men is chief among them. Christians have also suffered by the unjust legacies of the millet system, enduring systematic suffering for their faith.[21] This suffering is difficult: rulers have, at times, offered some shelter and protection to Christians and, to some degree, that is admirable and good. Yet, it has been suicidal for Christians to put their faith in rulers for security and privilege, offering them allegiance to the neglect of their love of neighbour, and displaying a willingness to quietly tolerate the proud, violent arrogance of autocratic rulers.

Synod?

We must also give attention to the ways our churches and its leaders relate to political power, in light of the threefold offices of Jesus: Prophet, Priest and King. We as Christians in our faith community are likewise tasked with this threefold commission: first, offering prophetic witness, upholding the Word of God in our lives and land; second, offering priestly roles, in extending the good news of Jesus's sacrifice for the world; and third, pointing at all times to the kingship of Jesus and the reality of the kingdom of God. Yet church leadership has often surrendered its prophetic and priestly voice in exchange for its own security and privileges. The temptations to acquire power are great, and constant; Jesus himself was so tempted. Sadly, this political power is also used as a way to control these leader's own Christian communities. We are not called to be of the world.

We must be called to confession – a confession of King Jesus.

Of course, the confession we make to, for and in the public realm is not for "us," and often does not lead to greater security and privilege for our Christian communities. When we fail to orientate our lives upon our risen Lord, and instead make our own privilege and security paramount, we also fail to live our commission as Christ's ambassadors. So, as citizens of the kingdom of God, we reject the tempting foolishness of a limited and passing security or privilege for the greater good and reality of an eternal kingdom with unsurpassable riches. For the sake of our neighbours, we commit to working for proximate, temporal political solutions that advance what the kingdom of God values: justice, mercy, love for neighbour and provision for all. When a society operates in humble righteousness, everyone benefits, including Christians.

Our modern nation-states are suffering, and so are the people living within them. The state systems are struggling or simply failing to offer social services and security. They face the threat of political instability not just from transnational actors, but also from the cancers of corruption and repression. Christians today have a unique opportunity to offer meaning, belonging, protection, provision and witness to the greater reality of the kingdom of God.

---

21. See Andrews, *Identity Crisis*, 56–64.

The church must serve, not just in liturgy and prayer, but also in living as an actual community, holding fast to what is good and true for human flourishing, and offering a welcome to those outside.

Our churches need to give serious thought to, and teach on questions related to, political theology: how to engage with those who rule, both in the midst of the dominant, "ruling" culture and also with those who are officially charged with the duties of governance, justice and the sword. The apostle Paul exhorts believers to pray for those in governance (e.g. 1 Tim 2:1–2). These are rugged, reality-based intercessions: for endurance, righteousness, the just treatment of the marginalized, for constraints on the temptations and corruptions of power and for evil to be thwarted – all as we await the peace of the coming kingdom.

8

Media in the Mission of God

We move in this chapter to look at the use of media by Christians in the Middle East. This includes printing and distributing books, leaflets and magazines, broadcasting radio and TV, the distribution of videos, and in more recent decades, various online methods. Whilst much was initiated by those from outside the region, increasingly media work has been by and for people of the region. It has allowed Middle Eastern Christians to express their faith to their communities and nations.

We had a brief glimpse of this in chapter 1 with the Jesus Film *and* Damascus Speaks, *about the life of Paul. The former was produced outside of the region and subsequently dubbed into Arabic and other Middle Eastern languages. In contrast,* Damascus Speaks *was written and produced in Arabic.*

Our thoughts are led by Ashraf Bacheet (see contributors' bios) assisted by Samah Fakhreldein.

Background: A Survey of Media in the Middle East (by Samah Fakhreldein)

Christians have been engaged in various forms of media for many years. Historically, this started with print media, then radio, followed by television and then online.

Print media, notably Bible translation and distribution, has been part of regular activity for centuries. During the 1970s a group of Christians in Beirut introduced a Christian magazine, *Huwa wa Hiya,* aimed at the mass market. The Lebanese Civil War (see appendix) prompted a change of location, with the team moving to Cairo. The magazine ran for approximately thirty years and was distributed in much of the MENA region. Its demise was the result of technological and sociological change.

Christian radio ministry began in the early twentieth century with Arabic Christian programmes on Western radio stations such as *Hawl al Alaam*, *Sawt el Injeil* and others that made use of shortwave radio. These stations provided a great opportunity for audiences to listen to the gospel regardless of location or background. These stations developed a system for listeners to send their questions about the Christian faith by post, and they allocated people to respond to the mail they received. Over time, such services were complemented by telephone, email, text and online chat rooms. With time, fully independent Christian radio stations were established within the Middle East, like radio *Sawt al Mahabba* in Lebanon in 1984. Each had full-time teams producing Christian programmes.[1]

One observation about Christian radio in its early days was that international shortwave stations were typically listened to by educated, unemployed, single men. Consequently, where groups of new believers emerged, their membership comprised mostly such people. This phenomenon profoundly shaped the indigenous church as it emerged across several North African countries. In the twenty-first century this effect is much reduced because the audiences of local FM stations are typically more in line with the population demographic.

Another massive technological jump came in the 1990s when the first Christian television stations were launched. The potential audience was much higher since most families in the MENA region owned at least one television set and satellite channels had become very popular following the Gulf War of 1991 (see appendix). In contrast to shortwave radio, the proliferation of satellite broadcasting gave families the opportunity to witness authentic Christian life through their television screens. In 2016 there were fourteen Christian satellite channels broadcasting in the Arab world.[2]

In 1991, *Tele Lumiere* was established as the first Christian television channel in Lebanon. Initially it was owned and operated as a secular channel, before being brought under the supervision of the Lebanese Council of the Catholic Patriarchs and Bishops. Subsequently, it became *Nour Sat* satellite channel. Additional Christian satellite channels currently broadcasting in the region belong to Orthodox, Protestant and Catholic denominations, while some channels identify themselves as ecumenical.

---

1. www.kreimmediacenter.org/ (accessed 19 December 2018).

2. Sara Afshari, *Christian Media in the Middle East: An Introduction,* 5 August 2016, http://christian-orient.eu/2016/08/05/christliche-medien-im-nahen-osten-eine-einfuehrung/?lang=en (accessed 13 September 2016).

Christian satellite channels play an important role in Christian education, elucidating the Christian faith and providing positive examples of Christian life. In addition, they play a great role in outreach to non-Christians and raise awareness of common causes in the Arab societies. Some channels, however, seek to highlight the Christian role in the public life in response to a growing sense of marginalization within the Arab world. Christian broadcasting is responsible for presenting voices of hope and courage, restoring the forgotten history of Christianity within the cultures of the MENA region, and discipling Christ's followers.

One broad classification is between those channels that operate within the region and those that are based outside. Typically, the former provides a positive presentation of Christianity with little, if any, critique of other faiths or political leaders. In contrast, some of those based outside the region take an overtly polemical stance, providing insightful and deeply challenging critiques of Islam. Any channel with operations inside the region that did this would most likely find its indigenous facilities either closed down by the authorities or attacked by extremists.

The socio-political situation in the region following the Arab Spring (see appendix) has affected the broadcast strategies of some Christian satellite channels. For example, they are much more able to engage in discussion-type programmes about current affairs. An academic study by Cambridge Arab Media Project assesses this development by examining two Christian channels, *al Hayat* and *Coptic Television Channel* (CTC).[3]

The *al Hayat* channel has faced some tough criticism from within the Arab world as a result of its polemical discourse on the Islamic faith. The strategy of *al Hayat* has been to search for the shortcomings, deficiencies and imperfections in Islam in order to convince Muslims to convert to Christianity. In doing so, they seek to present a "complete" Christian faith in contrast to the "limitations" of Islam. Many of the presenters are converts from a Muslim background. One of the station's programmes was hosted by a Coptic Orthodox priest who focused on religious polemics with the aim of proving the supremacy of Christianity over Islam. On the other hand, *al Hayat* has another programme hosted by a Moroccan convert from Islam who discusses subjects like the status of minorities under the rule of Islamic Law. At least one Islamic satellite

---

3. Cambridge Arab Media Project (CAMP) (ed.) *Religious Broadcasting in the Middle East: Islamic, Christian and Jewish Channels: Programmes and discourses* (University of Cambridge, 2010) www.med-media.eu/wp-content/uploads/2014/07/cambridge_media_report.pdf (accessed 9 December 2018).

channel has been established specifically to counter *al Hayat*; evidence that Christian media fuels change in the region.

In contrast, two channels operating from within the region are CTC and SAT-7. We will meet the latter in the case studies. CTC was established in 2007 and seeks to build bridges and establish peaceful relationships with Muslims, often congratulating Muslims on their religious occasions. It broadcasts rituals and prayers, making its Orthodox character very clear. It also has programming that articulates Orthodox doctrine, including being clear about where this differs from Protestant teaching.

The emergence of the internet created new opportunities for Christian media. Existing organizations made their material available online. Bible distribution had a new means. Radio and television channels added online streaming to complement their broadcasting.

In addition to these developments, many new Christian websites have been established which focus on presenting Christian educational content in addition to direct contact with users through email and online chatrooms. One example is the Arabic Bible Outreach Ministry[4] which focuses on spreading the gospel in the Middle East through the internet and offers audio and video content for free.

Another example is the St Takla Haymanout Coptic Orthodox website associated with the Coptic Orthodox church in Egypt. Its focus is to serve the church around the world to "always be prepared to give an answer to everyone who asks you to give the reason for the hope that you have."[5] This website introduces Christian educational tools and apologetics materials. It also introduces Coptic Orthodox rituals and creeds.

Another example is the social media project I Share Life – Young Christians Online in the Middle East, initiated by the Christian NGO Open Doors.[6] Its aim is "to see a new generation of young Christians seeking innovative ways to share their lives with Christ online through social media and sharing his love in a region torn apart by conflicts, violence, and despair."[7] They have an online support team operating from within the region which interacts with visitors. They record high levels of daily interactions on their Facebook pages as well as deeper conversations leading to in-depth, heart-to-heart ministry.

---

4. http://ar.arabicbible.com (accessed 29 August 2018).

5. http://st-takla.org (accessed 29 August 2018).

6. "The world's largest outreach to persecuted Christians in the most high-risk places." www.opendoors.org (accessed 11 January 2019)

7. https://opendoorsinternational.exposure.co/i-share-life (accessed 29 August 2018).

The advent of social media represents another significant revolution in Christian media outreach. With an abundance of social media platforms, the world is more interconnected than ever before – allowing the peoples of the Middle East unprecedented access to the gospel message. About half of the people living in the Middle East are estimated to have access to the Internet. The greatest example of the collective impact of social media is the Arab Spring, largely fuelled by online media.[8] Professor Damian Radcliffe's fourth annual report titled *Social Media in the Middle East: The Story of 2015* notes that there are more than 41 million active users in the region using different platforms.[9]

The general goal is to see people engaged not only in an online Christian community, but wherever possible also in an offline community – a local church (see chapter 2). Numerous online social-media based Christian ministries have emerged, a reflection of the role of online media in our contemporary world. This causes us to ask the questions: what does it look like to be a social media-minded community of faith? Also, what are the next steps for the church given recent revolutions in information technology? These questions are explored in the following case studies and reflections.

Editorial Reflection

Two observations emerge from the above. First, the contrast between use of media to reach the region as a whole, for example the magazine and satellite television, and use for very specific groups within this broad context. Radio illustrates this with shortwave being regional and FM more local. Where the former is obliged to use widely understood forms of Arabic, the latter uses the dialect of the intended audience. Satellite television is very broad, as are some social media. Yet, other social media are very focused.

Second, the sensitive issue of who is in control. Much use of media was initiated by outsiders, missionaries. Very quickly they engaged indigenous Christians. Over time, control of agenda and content moved from the internationals to the nationals. The advent of audience-specific media has necessitated a similar transition, this time from Arab Christian to Arabs of Muslim background. Wayne Larson, International Director of Middle East Media,[10] explained that in order to target the content appropriately, it is best if

---

8. www.exministries.com/social-media-projects-influence-middle-east-for-christ/ (accessed 19 December 2018).

9. https://damianradcliffe.files.wordpress.com/2016/01/social-media-in-the-middle-east-2015-review-damian-radcliffe.pdf (accessed 19 December 2018).

10. www.mem.org/ (accessed 26 November 2018).

it is created by those from the intended audience. Furthermore, these Muslim-background producers need to stay in or very close to their communities. Why? Because if they moved away they would quickly lose the subtle nuances of their audience due to the rapid rate of change. The implication is that believers from Muslim backgrounds must be encouraged to remain wherever possible, seeing migration in general, and emigration from the region in particular, as their option of last resort.[11]

Case Studies: Media's Calling, A Journey through Middle Eastern Lives (by Samah Fakhreldein)

Our case studies look at three people whose full-time work is in Christian media. One is Lebanese and two are Egyptian; for all three their work is region-wide. The first focuses on supporting and equipping indigenous Christians, while the other two focus on evangelism and the discipleship of Jesus's followers from Muslim backgrounds.

A Remarkable Dreamer Rises from a Civil War

Rita el Mounayer is a senior member of SAT-7.[12] "My story is like that of many Lebanese. When I was a little girl living through the violence of the Civil War (see appendix), we slept in bomb shelters. During that time, television cartoons were our only refuge from the horrors going on around us. Since then, I began to dream about joining the world of media in order to bring the joy I received to other children."

Rita started her media career as a radio host and producer with Far East Broadcasting Association (FEBA) radio in 1992. With this experience, she joined SAT-7 from its formation in 1995. The channel launched in 1996 with a two-hour broadcast once a week. Rita hosted her first children's programme, *al Sanabel* (Ears of Wheat), a programme that aired for twelve years and was one of the channel's most successful shows.

---

11. See Andrews, *Last Resort*; and Stephen Carter, "Staying for Good: 113 Middle Eastern Christians and the Challenge to Remain," in Sam George and Miriam Adenay, eds., *Refugee Diasporas: Missions amid the Greatest Humanitarian Crisis of Our Times* (Pasadena: William Carey Publishing, 2018).

12. See http://sat7.org/about-us/our-mission (accessed 29 August 2018).

Rita's role expanded from that of host and producer of children's programmes to becoming programming director for all of the Arabic programming from 2004 onwards.

Rita's background and experience with the Lebanese Civil War were her main motivations for her involvement in the launching of the first independent Arabic Christian channel for children. She remarked, "I wanted to share with them the joy I had when I was a child from cartoons, while also broadcasting hope in Christ." This dream came true in 2007 with the launching of SAT-7 KIDS, a second Arabic language channel exclusively for children.

SAT-7 is a strategic satellite television service for the people of the Middle East and North Africa. Rita notes that "SAT-7 covers the western half of the 10/40 Window (see glossary), which is identified by missiologists as the least reached area in the world. It is a region in unprecedented crisis, increasing instability and illiteracy. We are aware of the needs of this region. That is why we maintain production centres in multiple Middle Eastern countries, as we recognize the importance of locally-made programmes and of the local church's involvement in this." Rita observes that when SAT-7 was formed it was very hard to find qualified believers to work at the station. This has changed; expertise is increasingly available in many Arab countries.

SAT-7 is supported by multiple agencies and inter-denominational partnerships, with a unique network of partners operating telephone counselling and audience follow-up centres. She continued: "We are not replacing the church; we just plant the seed and work with the church. We are Arab Christians who live in the MENA region, so 80 percent of our programming is indigenously made by Middle Eastern Christians in order to equip more local leaders from the MENA context."

To which she added that they do not follow the normal model of Christian broadcasting by selling their airtime to other ministries. Rather, they plan their broadcast schedules because they intentionally do not want to give the impression that Christianity is a Western religion. They aim to instill a sense of belonging among their Arab viewers. She pointed out that in the 1990s the station could not transmit from the Egyptian owned Nile Sat satellite; they were obliged to use "Hot Bird" and other European-owned satellites. In 2010 they were allowed to broadcast from Nile Sat, a sign of growing acceptance of the station's programming within the region.

When asked why she is so passionate about her work with SAT-7, Rita responded by saying, "From the beginning, the foundation of SAT-7 has shown respect to others, even if we disagree with them. As a result, our programming is politically and culturally sensitive, and it never attacks another faith nor political institutions."

This strategy has added great value to Rita's dream of transforming Arab societies and to living in a peaceful atmosphere where people from different sects can sit together at the reconciliation table.

In the years following the Arab Spring (see glossary) and with the rise of new political movements, SAT-7 programming began to carry different messages, including love, forgiveness and turning the other cheek. They hope to influence Christians to put their faith into practice by doing good things in society and being sure about their faith. Through their broadcasts, it is apparent that SAT-7 promotes social justice by motivating Christians to reach out to those on the margins of society. As part of this, in 2017 they inaugurated an additional channel, SAT-7 Academy, specifically providing educational programming for displaced children unable to attend regular schooling.

As for the children's ministry, Rita said,

> I have a passion for children because I believe they are the future of the Arab world. They are going to change the society. They are going to talk to their siblings and to their friends and to their family about the love of God. You see people in the Arab world using media to shape the hearts and minds of children from an early age. You see a lot of programmes interrupted for the call to prayer, Qur'anic verses and messages of hate and violence – especially on certain television stations in the Middle East. However, we broadcast cartoons, dramas, Bible stories and game shows which attract children and help them learn about God's love for them and demonstrate how they can walk with Jesus.

Their message addresses not only the children, but the entire family as parents sit down with their children while they receive a message of love. Rita believes that if we want to change the face of Arab society, we have to start with children. One day, the children who grew up watching and being influenced by SAT-7 will become the leaders of their nations.

A Leader from the Margins

Khalil has been a friend to many converts from Islam over the years, assisting them step by step during the early stages of their faith journey with Christ. He enables many to find a small group in their town for further discipleship and the living out of their newfound faith. Khalil has dedicated many years of his life to this ministry, in response to God's call for him to love and serve "other sheep" (see John 10:16).

When asked about the reason for his passion to reach "other sheep," as he describes them, Khalil replied that, "the call came to my life gradually. I was a typical Egyptian Christian, a traditional believer who moved to find a job in Saudi Arabia. At that time I came to see the world with different eyes. If I felt that Christians in Egypt are marginalized, in Saudi I experienced true oppression, where Christians have no rights at all."

He continued,

> I worked in a store. Each time I heard the call to prayer, I had two options: either close the store and go home or go to the mosque to pray. When I refused to do either, the police came to my store, insulted me and took my passport. When I went to the police office to retrieve my passport, I found myself in a long queue of those with similar cases. Finally, when I met with the officer, he put his shoes on my face and he asked why I did not go to the mosque to pray. I told him that I am a Christian, whereupon he yelled at me, called me an infidel and threw all the passports out of the window. Together with more than two hundred others I went into the street and spent many hours trying to find mine. I asked myself why they hated us so much and began to feel there was something wrong. I felt they needed to experience the love of Jesus, but I did not know how I could show them that love.
>
> I decided to move back from Saudi Arabia to Egypt. I started working at a media recording studio. It was at this time God called me to leave my job and dedicate my life to ministry. I tried to ignore that call, but then one day one of our customers – a Saudi Sheikh – came to me and asked me to record the Qur'an for him. He wanted to distribute it all over the world so that everyone could hear about and follow Islam. I felt in my heart that I could not do this. I took this as a sign from God to follow his call. I knew then that I had to share the gospel with the whole world. So, I quit my job and started my ministry, trying to reach "the other sheep," using all available media tools on the internet or television. I started to work with Christian television, providing follow-up counselling for those who call audience response telephone numbers. Eventually, I began our own website.

Khalil serves as Executive Director for *Maarifa* (knowledge),[13] a website for people from different backgrounds and nationalities to learn more about Jesus, his teachings and the Christian faith. The website focuses on people from age fifteen to thirty-five, but serves all who access it. He and his team receive calls from audience members of various Christian television channels. The follow-up ministry is available to callers around the clock with a qualified team ready to deal with a caller's needs, from theology to personal counselling.

Critical to this ministry is the communication skills of the counsellor answering calls. As such, Khalil works with a professional and dedicated team ready to receive calls at any time, answering questions related to spirituality and faith. When they feel a person with whom they are speaking has come to faith in Jesus, they proceed to walk with them through a journey of discipleship. When they feel a person is ready, they connect them with the nearest group of local believers. They have had applications for discipleship in twelve Arabic dialects.

Most of those to whom they minister are from Saudi Arabia, the Gulf and North Africa. So we can say that part of Khalil's dream has become a reality. Many of these "other sheep" are now joining the flock, and he hopes that one day they will reshape MENA society.

Sleeping Vision Comes to Reality

Ashraf Bacheet is the regional director for the online ministry Christian Vision (CV) through which he fulfils his long-standing vision to share the gospel with ordinary people using social media and the Internet.

He explains that he is

> an Egyptian man from a Coptic Orthodox background who accepted Jesus when I was in my twenties. Since then, I have had a passion to share what Jesus did in my life with others: I see how my life has changed, and I desire to share that change with others by all available means. I worked in different professions, including managing an advertising agency during which I learned a lot about media. In 2000, I went through a very difficult time: I was sick and my business collapsed, prompting me to reflect upon my life. In a personal message, God told me to reach the nations, reconciling them with himself through the good news that they might know his Son Jesus Christ.

---

13. www.Maarifa.org (accessed 26 November 2018).

This vision took me ten years to start, but I felt during these ten years that God was preparing me for ministry. I had a clear word from God to use some sort of media, which I could not understand at that time, but which he identified as "new" media. That terminology was not used in the year 2000 to describe social media or the Internet, but God described to me through a few verses how he wanted to connect us all. I wrote this in my journal.

Ashraf was connected with CV in 2008 when they were shifting their focus from being a shortwave radio ministry to operating exclusively online. They asked him to produce a report covering the MENA region about how they might expand their remit to include use of the Arabic language. He said, "They were shifting from traditional media to new media, where I have my calling and passion." In 2010 they established a small team in the Middle East to start ministry in the Arabic language. Their first project was sharekonline.com,[14] an Arabic language and MENA contextualized version of their website yesHEis.com.[15] Ashraf describes this project as a powerful tool to help Christians share the gospel online with their non-believer friends in a way that is as natural and enjoyable as everything else they do on social media. It is both a web and mobile application.

CV intentionally uses simple, non-Christian terminology in all their audio and video materials, language that people from any background can understand. Ashraf explained, "we use short, high quality videos and materials which are visually attractive. So, when anyone shares them on his or her page, they will get a certain link. Then, if they want to continue, they receive another link allowing them to watch the salvation message introduced by a youth pastor. We present the gospel in many different Arabic accents, allowing our viewers to interact more naturally with the message." Ashraf describes this as a completely safe and secure tool.

Ashraf's second project is sawtonline.org.[16] Ashraf explains that, "after the Arab Spring erupted in 2011, we started to observe that in many MENA countries an increasing number of outspoken atheists were using social media to freely proclaim that God does not exist." Ashraf and his team tried to find resources in Arabic to help them to resist this trend, but everything they found was in English. As a result, they decided to make their own resources and present them online. Thus sawtonline.org was born. From the feedback

---

14. www.sharekonline.com/ (accessed 26 November 2018).

15. yesHEis.com (accessed 26 November 2018).

16. www.sawtonline.org/ (accessed 26 November 2018).

received, they found that Saudi Arabians and Algerians were the most interested and active nationalities on this website.

In addition, sawtonline.org produce webpages related to a variety of different topics, including harassment, addiction, homosexuality and suicide. The technical jargon is "landing pages," meaning content designed to be found by those searching for material on a specific subject. Ashraf notes that "the MENA region has some of the highest rates of such social problems in the world, and this is a source of shame in our societies." Once more, we see Christians seeking to transform society.

According to Ashraf, the primary challenges faced by his ministries relate to "church leadership and state governments. Many church leaders are not equipped to cope with our contemporary age. Older leaders typically suffer from an inability to reach out to the youth. They use traditional tools of ever decreasing effect and are perceived as being irrelevant to ordinary people. With regard to the governments, what we do is perceived as evangelism. This is a crime that can put those with whom we interact in a very critical situation. There is a huge security challenge."

Concluding Reflection

The above models show us how God is using media in a variety of remarkable ways to disciple Christians and reach out to non-Christians. They show us how God is bringing in "the other sheep," using new patterns to reshape Arab societies and reconcile us with himself through his Son, Jesus Christ, our Saviour. Having met Ashraf, he now provides our reflection, which picks up on his observation above about security issues; how can we be "as shrewd as snakes and as innocent as doves" (Matt 10:16)?

Missiological Reflection: Opportunities and Dangers Online (by Ashraf Bacheet)

There was a rise in the number of converts from Islam to Christianity in the 1980s and 1990s, which coincided with the start of Christian mass media channels. This began with Monte Carlo Radio, followed by other shortwave radio channels. Christian satellite television channels were pioneered by SAT-7 and followed by many others. Each time a new technology was adopted by the church then a new surge in conversions was observed. Furthermore, since social media was utilized by Christians to proclaim their faith another sustained surge of people choosing to follow Jesus has been observed. But how far can this go? Does media really have the potential to win back the Middle East and North Africa for Christ?!

For the media we produce today to be effective, they must be relevant and engaging. Storytelling is the most effective strategy in today's busy media scene, where enormous amounts of information are competing for everyone's limited attention span. Jesus and Paul both brilliantly contextualized the gospel message to their audiences.

Acts 17:16–34 describes the Apostle Paul's visit to Athens where he caused controversy by preaching a contextualized gospel message. We could paraphrase his approach as asking, "What do people worship here? What is trending/popular here? That is what I want to talk to you about and explain how Jesus could transform your situation." His approach led to churches being planted and new believers discipled in Athens and wherever else he went.

We need to learn from the past, aware that some Christian leaders used to urge their congregations not to watch TV. We need to avoid similar failures to appreciate the positive, creative use of new technologies in *missio Dei*. The gospel is the most creative story in history: it can and must be shown on media. What about these times? Should we look at church-planting opportunities on social media instead of in physical spaces? Should we embrace online church and *Skypleship*? This is a new term referring to online discipleship using video conferencing tools such as Skype.

Technology today allows us to specifically target a segment of audience based on their interests, demographics and behaviour. We should always design our communications and tell our stories with specific persona in mind. How can we create effective media content in this context?

Fuelled by the rise of social media as a news source, and a growing distrust of facts offered by the establishment, post-truth as a concept has been finding its linguistic footing for some time. I would not be surprised if post-truth becomes one of the defining terms of our time.[17] On the other hand, social media tries to dictate to us how to live life and define our present era, referred to as post-post-modern era by some. No one is just a passive audience; everyone can participate. All sorts of ideas are expressed as content, distributed for free, go viral and shape the next trend in politics, art or even belief. Everyone is engaged in this process, either by creating these trends or consuming them. The Arab Spring is an example.

The history and the future of radio are very interesting. I do believe that people will continue to listen to audio-based media and probably more than

---

17. http://engagingmedia.info/media-post-truth-world/ (accessed 26 November 2018).

ever in the coming years. I believe that audio often has more opportunities than video because it can be consumed in a passive way. For instance, you can listen to music while you work out or a podcast while you drive. Video requires the attention of your eyes and ears where audio media only requires your ears. I see all our devices talking to each other and allowing us to easily move from one place to another and continue to engage with the same piece of media. Currently this happens by putting your phone on speaker, but the future will be much more immersive and natural.

On the other hand, podcasting sounds simple and compared to historical shortwave radio it is. The reality is that it still requires a lot of hard work to create content, capture and edit the content, optimize the material for distribution, grow the audience and keep adjusting to the constant changes in technology.

Video apps can help churches reach more people effectively through cutting-edge technology. Such tools can be expensive and complicated, but they do not have to be. We can create resources that are powerful, flexible and align with the mission of the church. Video apps can serve as an online church campus, in a prison, or serving those in countries where it is illegal to have church buildings or conventional church services. (*We looked at the composition of church services in chapter 2.*)

While content is king, marketing is everything. When you are looking for something where is the first place that you go? Google, of course. Google offers non-profit organizations anywhere in the world a significant monthly amount of free Adwords advertising. YouTube is the main global video distribution platform for video and there are numerous options for churches when it comes to creating content specifically for YouTube. Using sermons as content or posting clips of sermons or capturing interviews with your pastor can do well on YouTube. I believe the best content on this platform though, is content specifically made for it. Creating videos specifically for YouTube requires understanding the significance of this being the second most widely used search engine in the world; we need to think clearly about who we are seeking to reach and what they might be searching for.

Virtual reality and augmented reality are the most creative expressions of media we have experienced to date. How can such disruptive technological innovations be utilized for ministry? One approach is by implementing "lean startup"[18] methodologies which comprise research on observing lead-users' behaviour, intentionally nurturing the incubation and acceleration process

---

18. http://theleanstartup.com (accessed 26 November 2018).

of innovative media ventures and setting clear metrics and key performance indicators relevant for mission. Unfortunately, there is no short-cut.

It is clear that technology has strengthened the work of Christian ministries around the world. However, we must be wise in considering the full implications of the rapid adoption of so many electronic devices and online services. One aspect of the use of technology in the missional context is that of cyber security. It is important to note that I can provide only a "point in time" perspective: internet security is changing rapidly, both in terms of the types of risks and the potential solutions to address the challenges.

Cyber security deals with unauthorized or unexpected access to data and electronic devices. Such access can expose identities of seekers, field workers, budgets, methods and physical locations. I have observed mission organizations applying excellent practice and also those not paying enough attention to online security. One question that all organizations must ask – even if they do not want to ask it openly – is "what is the compelling reason for us to invest a lot of resources in this problem?" The potential for serious problems must be visible to senior leaders, boards and donors, who all have an interest in – and a duty to – reduce organizational risk.

During 2017 a survey was conducted of some MENA region missional organizations which gathered information about the impact of cyber security breaches, as well as the practices, attitudes and aspirations about cyber security.[19] The results of this survey indicated that cyber breaches were having a deep and costly impact on many organizations. While it is not possible to provide comprehensive cyber-risk mitigation guidance in this book, the survey highlighted the necessity for basic mitigation. We can, though, give a summary of the consequences seen, which include the expulsion of expatriate Christians, loss of organizational reputation, the loss of time and resources, and the closure by the authorities of some activities. More serious has been the arrest and imprisonment of national and expatriate Christians. Worse still are cases of the murder of indigenous Christians and of non-Christians exploring the claims of Christ.

This type of loss actually meets the definition of a genuine "cyber war."[20]

Christian ministry organizations need to consider reducing their cyber risk in an approachable and affordable way. One starting place is the core cyber

---

19. This is the *MII Cyber Security Report – 2017*. It is not made public.

20. One definition is encapsulated in the line: "'Cyber war' is over hyped: it ain't war till someone dies."

security profile we are describing here which fits within the first five Critical Security Controls of the Center for Internet Security.[21]

Such considerations should not deter us from using media, including online approaches. We do, though, need to be wise, vigilant, and aware of the potential risks, and who is most likely to bear the consequences of unwise actions and practices.

The church needs to keep moving forward, or else the past will become our destination. Science and technology keep pushing humanity forward and by the time this book is published (and even much more by the time you read it) new technologies will have erupted and some Christians will be waiting for someone to assist them into the ministry where they will be involved in providing innovative methods of furthering God's kingdom.

Who will accept the challenge and become the next innovator for Christ?

Editorial Reflection: Who Reaps the Consequences?

The reference to security issues prompts a reflection on some of our terminology and behaviour. This section is written by a Westerner addressing fellow Westerners.

Many of us use the terms "secret believer" and "underground church," meaning someone who hides their decision to follow Christ and a church meeting discreetly in a location not recognized legally as a place of worship. These terms are simplistic, one or the other, black and white. For individual believers from Muslim backgrounds, it is more nuanced to ask who knows about their following Jesus, who does not, and how is this changing over time. This allows disclosure to be done based on relationship.

Withstanding that, given the capability of information technology, we must start to question whether there are contexts in which these terms can no longer be wisely applied. Online monitoring, data-capture and data-mining techniques enable those companies and authorities with the motivation and means to gather profiles of individuals with remarkable accuracy. Most governments in the Arab world have the motivation and some undoubtedly have the means, for example the Gulf States. The prevalence of security cameras in some places means that the movement of individuals and groups can be tracked by those governments with the means to do so. In such places, we need

---

21. www.sans.org/security-resources/posters/special/20-critical-security-controls-55 (accessed 26 November 2018).

to be aware that individuals and groups that identify with Jesus and become his adherents can be identified as such.

Those of us who support the church in the MENA region need to be careful about how we communicate with and about our brothers and sisters. It is they who reap the consequences of our words and deeds.

It is exciting to see many coming to know Jesus as Saviour and Lord. Like many, I rejoice in the numerical growth of God's kingdom. Yet, I have seen severe trouble come to some new communities of Christians because widespread attention was given to them in the West. Often this has been initiated by those of the same nationality with residency in Western countries. In one country in the Arab world it prompted the enacting of new legislation governing non-Muslim worship, legislation that has been used against emerging Christian congregations and communities.

One organization that I know had a board-level discussion about their fund-raising strategy. The needs of those they served would be best served by being discreet; yet funding their activities would be best served by being more vocal about what they were doing. The chair concluded that the needs of those they served must take priority, recognizing that this made part of the ministry's work more difficult.

We should always keep in mind who is likely to reap the consequences of our actions. Media means that we live in a very interconnected world: what we do in the West affects our brothers and sisters in the MENA region.

9

Children and Youth in the Mission of God

This chapter looks at the younger people amongst the peoples of the Middle East. Earlier chapters have referred to this age group, notably one of the case studies in chapter 8. The demographics of the Middle East make this a particularly crucial age group to address. Arab world youth are part of the global youth culture that has arisen from modern technology, starting with satellite television and amplified by online services, especially social media. The as yet unmet aspirations of the Arab Spring make these generations especially critical to the future of the lands they have been born into.

The background section gives us a historical overview, as well as introducing the theme that Jesus welcomed children and that some of his first disciples were young. Our two case studies involve people whose experience of youth work as teenagers was a precursor to their roles as leaders in youth work as adults. The missiological reflection asks several probing questions concerning the place within churches of youth: are they tolerated or accepted as contributing members? Youth are the present of the church, not just its future, just as they were for Jesus.

Our thoughts are guided by Nabil Habiby, aided by Melanie Baggao and Samah Fakhreldein (see contributors' bios).

Background: "Let the Little Children Come to Me" (by Melanie Baggao)

Jesus said, "Let the little children come to me, and do not hinder them, for the kingdom of heaven belongs to such as these" (Matt 19:14).

Veiled at the age of twelve, Fatima entered the group of other youth singing songs about a man named Jesus. Cradling the scars of her war-torn life in Syria, she acknowledged a peaceful feeling in her heart as she sang.

It is not unusual to hear of experiences such as Fatima's among children. God tenderly cares for children and even encourages adults to be like them (e.g. Matt 18:2–5). The Bible records numerous examples of children and youth who are not only blessed by the mission of God but are also active in being a part of God's mission on earth. Throughout the history of God's mission in the Middle East, one can find these very same standards: children and youth continue to challenge the church in living out the mission of God.

The ancient world was not a friendly place for children, particularly orphans. However, the church was known for its radical love for the poor, orphans and widows. David Z. Nowell claims that, "Virtually every early writing on Christian conduct stressed the importance of caring for children without parents. Eusebius, the Apostolic Constitutions, Lactantius, Ignatius, Polycarp, Justin Martyr . . . the list goes on and on, but every one of them called on the early church to care for orphans."[1] The providers put the injunctions of Scripture into practice as they cared for these children.

Many Western evangelical Christians are familiar with the "10/40 Window" (see glossary) as an area of the world with the least access to the gospel and Christian resources. A less well-known term is the "4–14 window." The 4–14 Window Movement describes the focus on child evangelism between the ages of four and fourteen. This "window" of receptivity to the gospel is based on research done by American George Barna which shows that "children between the ages of five and thirteen have a 32 percent probability of accepting Jesus Christ as their Saviour."[2] Children and youth in the Middle East are in both these "windows."

The 4–14 missiology seeks to place children and youth as active participants in the mission of God. Instead of viewing children as simply "objects of mission,"

---

1. David Z. Nowell, *Dirty Faith: Bringing the Love of Christ to the Least of These* (Bloomington: Bethany House, 2014).

2. John W. Kennedy, "The 4–14 Window: New Push on Child Evangelism Targets the Crucial Early Years," *Christianity Today* 48, no. 7 (Jul 2004): 53.

new initiatives and strategies encourage children to be "agents for mission."[3] The thrust of young people being a part of God's mission is not new to the MENA region. It was in this region that God first displayed the fulfilment of his mission through youth in the Bible. Some biblical examples include Samuel hearing and responding to God's call, Josiah bringing great reform as a boy king, David practising courage before Goliath, Jonathan's willingness to risk his life for his friend and the boy with five loaves and two fish (John 6:9).[4]

In the eighteenth and nineteenth centuries, education was one area of ministry many foreign mission agencies working in the region delved into. The most popular were The American Board of Commissioners for Foreign Missions and the UK's Church Missionary Society, now called the Church Mission Society (CMS). In Lebanon, Syria, and Turkey:

> . . . missionaries soon felt the need for establishing primary schools, and later secondary ones, to enable their local followers to persist in their faith and to learn to read and write, especially to be able to study the Bible. . . . One primary school after another was established in every town and village where they evangelized.[5]

In Egypt, CMS "strove to spread the Bible and to teach the Christian faith to younger people in order to revive the Coptic church."[6] Schools for boys and girls were established in Cairo, Assyut and the Suez Canal region. One of the shining achievements of these schools was the creation of the first school for girls in the Ottoman Empire during a time when society shunned female education.[7] These educational institutions led to the need for printing presses and higher education in the region, thus advancing the gospel in the region.

The First World War changed the climate of missionary endeavours in the Middle East. The war left over one hundred thousand children orphaned throughout the Ottoman Empire. Missionaries, monastic societies and charities were some of the first to respond, adding to the almost one hundred orphanages that they were running in 1914. After the massacres and expulsions of the Armenians in 1915, Christian organizations supported orphanages in Syria, Lebanon and Palestine. One of the "most effective and long-lasting American

---

3. Dan Brewster and John Baxter-Brown, eds., *Children and Youth as Partners in Mission* (Compassion International, 2013), 5. This is a compendium of papers presented at the 4/14 Window Missiology Conference held in Seoul, Korea, 26–28 February 2013.

4. Brewster and Baxter-Brown, *Children and Youth*, 60.

5. Badr, "Evangelical Missions," 717.

6. Badr, 736.

7. Habib Badr, "The Protestant Evangelical Community in the Middle East: Impact on Cultural and Societal Developments," *International Review of Mission* 89, no. 352 (Jan 2000): 61.

missionary responses" to the disasters of the First World War was the creation of Near East Relief.[8] This organization not only granted missionaries more opportunities for education as previous ministries had done, but also gave more attention to "economic development at the village level, medical services and assistance with orphans."[9] Again, one can see the mission of God expanding among orphans whose needs challenged the church to look beyond historical practices of education.

The pattern of being an agent of God's mission is not limited to relief for orphans, education initiated by foreign missionaries, or work only among evangelical circles in the region. In 1941, a group of Orthodox students met in Beirut and discussed the concerns they had about the state of their church. This led to The Beirut Conference in April 1955 when young Christians in the region held their first ecumenical meeting. Christian youth leaders of the Orthodox churches of Constantinople, Antioch, Cyprus and Greece, the Coptic, Armenian, Ethiopian and Syrian Orthodox churches, the evangelical and Anglican churches gathered to discuss Christian youth work in the Middle East. One of the key resolutions from the consultation included "the need for the spiritual renewal of youth in their churches" and a recognition of "the part they have to play in carrying out the mission of the church." In addition to improving the interrelationship among churches in the region, the consultation also encouraged Christian youth to have a greater understanding of those who share different beliefs in their own communities.[10] Like the examples set in the Bible, these young leaders took the initiative to foster a culture of youth participating in the mission of God in the region, an effect that endures to this day.

Today in the MENA region, children and youth make up two-thirds of the population.[11] For many, war continues to be a harsh reality or within living memory. The church continues to be moulded by the challenge to engage this next generation with the love of Christ. In the past, God has used children and youth across this region to challenge the body of Christ in following biblical examples, to help the church explore holistic ways to meet the needs of people and to encourage unity amongst the followers of Christ. "Because

---

8. Eleanor H. Tejirian and Reeva Spector Simon, *Conflict, Conquest, and Conversion* (New York: Columbia University Press, 2012), 179.

9. Tejirian and Simon, *Conflict, Conquest, and Conversion*, 92.

10. William A. Perkins, "Christian Youth in the Middle East," *The Ecumenical Review* 7, no. 4 (Jul 1955), 395.

11. See, for example, Suad Joseph, "The Future Today: Youth and Adolescents of the Middle East and North Africa," *Youth in the Arab World* (Nov 2011): 5.

of their energy, boldness, creativity and ingenuity, children have the capacity to mobilize immeasurable resources for the holistic transformation of their communities. Children and youth are some of the most valuable resources in the community."[12] New ways of reaching children and youth for the mission of God might include methods and practices the church has not considered, such as teaching Muslim background parents about how their children can choose Christ at an early age.[13] The mission of God among children and youth is not stagnant and God will continue to creatively bring new revelation to his church to not only bless young people with his love but also engage them in his work throughout the Middle East.

Case Studies (by Samah Fakhreldein)

What Is Planted in a Youth Might Impact a Nation

Maher Al Haj is a youth worker and the director of Youth for Christ (YFC) in Lebanon. He was born and raised in Saudi Arabia in a nominal Christian family. Maher recalls that, "I did not know anything about my faith, the Bible or Jesus while I was in Saudi Arabia. At age twelve my family moved back to Lebanon, and I discovered that I am a Christian, who belongs to a certain religion.[14] I started looking at what is Christianity as part of my exploration as a teenager about my identity. At that time, a school friend committed suicide, which prompted me to begin a spiritual journey looking for the meaning of the life because my friend's last note stated, 'life is meaningless and I prefer to die.'"

This event was life-changing for Maher; his journey was not only searching for identity but also trying to find a deep meaning for his life. Accordingly, he started to ask many questions of priests, pastors and other religious people, seeking logically reasonable answers that would satisfy his curiosity. "One of my friends invited me to a YFC programme during the Christmas period. I still remember the title of the event '24 crazy hours in the snow without sleep' and I wondered how they would run a programme for 24 hours without sleeping. I was attracted by the title of the event more than the people running it. I did not know anything about religion or the church; I thought they were boring and not relevant to young people. That night, I could say I met people who

---

12. Brewster and Baxter-Brown, *Children and Youth*, 82.

13. J. Dudley Woodberry, *From Seed to Fruit: Global Trends, Fruitful Practices, and Emerging Issues among Muslims* (Pasadena: William Carey Library, 2011), ebook.

14. For details of how all Middle Easterners are regarded as adherents of a specific religion see Andrews, *Identity Crisis*.

were followers of Christ." Maher was overwhelmed with the leaders' love, and his questions were answered from the Bible. "They had answers, and somehow the answers made sense. I started to read the Bible and attend their clubs, and later on, in 1994, I made my decision to follow Jesus."

Maher started working for YFC when he was a student as volunteer staff. Later, he became a full-time staff member, and in 2011 he became the director. "YFC has invested a lot in my life. They made me the leader that I am and the youth worker I am, and I do believe that my role is to invest in others. The purpose of finding meaning for life, gave me the motivation to help young people to find meaning for their lives. Those who have horrible lives, suicidal intentions and no clear future: these are the youth that I want to reach; these are the people that I want to share the gospel with. I want to tell them that there is hope, there is a meaning and there is an abundant life in Christ" (see John 10:10).

Maher is passionate about equipping indigenous youth workers in Lebanon and beyond. He is part of a team called Katalyst, a network of people involved in youth ministry across the Arab world. The goal of their gatherings is to train, empower and support youth workers. "The Lord appointed the right people to be in the Katalyst team. They gather two hundred leaders annually for fellowship, training and mutual exchange of experience."

The Katalyst ministry was a response to a huge need in the Arab church in disorienting times and contexts such as Iraq and Syria. These churches witnessed a huge amount of emigration to the West and elsewhere, causing a lack of experienced youth leaders. Maher and his team feel that they address this need by equipping new, emerging leaders, by building a network where they are able to share their experiences, and by supplying them with new Arabic resources and curricula.

The latter are provided by Maher and his team's creative writing projects. They partner with twenty youth workers from different Arab countries in special seminars to produce Arabic materials to fulfil the needs of the church for the youth.

Faith Encounter for the Leaders of the Future

Souhail is a youth leader. He worked in the business field before he was appointed the executive manager of an organization that runs summer camps in a Middle Eastern country. Souhail explained that, "You can call it an accident, but I see it as part of God's plan."

Souhail joined a new business where his boss was leading a ministry that serves the youth. In 2008, Souhail became a volunteer in this ministry, subsequently becoming a full-time employee. "This became a widely known ministry and I can regard it as a strong resource for new believers." This ministry works with those aged eight to eighteen. We do events in schools and summer camps in rural locations, applying a curriculum for the youth, including those who are not members of churches. "It is not only an evangelistic activity, we do a friendship bond, we walk with the teenagers in this critical period of their lives." He leads a team of a hundred and twenty volunteers who facilitate the summer camps and other activities throughout the year. Many of the volunteers were teenagers when they decided to be devout in following Jesus. Consequently, they know the challenges which face teenagers who want to follow Christ. "We share the message of Christ using modern tools in order to reach our highly demanding audiences. We choose an annual theme and develop a curriculum for it along with activities for each camp. It is hard because it consumes lots of time to research and develop tools according to different themes."

Souhail organizes and runs nine summer camps per year, plus numerous smaller gatherings for the leaders and volunteers throughout the year. The latter provide training on leadership skills, counselling and biblical knowledge. They also appoint new leaders each year from within the youth, whom they equip to join the leadership team. The team is well connected to the local church, engaging church leaders in developing the ministry, and using their advice to discern the needs of the youth within the church.

"This ministry started from the evangelical church, but became non-denominational to include multiple leaders from different churches. It is good to see the youth working together, as these activities might unite the church in the name of Christ. However, it is hard when some denominations seek to exploit this ministry for their own perceived advantage."

One of the main challenges Souhail faces is the lack of sufficient volunteers to act as mentors and facilitators. The core of the ministry is to have personal relationships, which requires great commitment from those who participate. Therefore, the absence of volunteers and the lack of time for follow-up are critical for the continuity of the ministry.

"One more challenge is when youth who do not belong to any church decide to follow Christ. Many churches are not fully equipped and ready to receive them."

Souhail's focus is on the uniqueness of each participant as they come from various levels within society, the poor and rich youth gather in a unity of

Christ. The youth who participate in the camps become a new community within society, where the different social levels and different backgrounds come along to meet with Christ.

Souhail has an annual tradition he does with every volunteer's training. He asks an important question: "Who gave their life to Christ during a camp?" and he says, "I always find half of the participants' hands are raised and my body shivers with joy." Souhail feels their success is mainly determined in one description, "A harvested youth helps to harvest more youth" because those who follow Jesus feel committed to ministry and become volunteers and mentors for others within the camps and beyond.

Missiological Reflection: Objects of or Participants in? (by Nabil Habiby)

This chapter reminds us that youth – meaning those aged under eighteen – are one of the main audiences of mission, the catalysts for innovation in mission, and participants in *missio Dei*.

On a philosophical level, post-modernism would cringe at the hint of brain-washing found in the triumphant claims of 4–14 missiology that not only "plucks" youth at an early age, but also engages them in further proselytizing. However, out of the same rejection of generalizations which post-modernism revels in, a logical response ensues: there is no such thing as youth in limbo, free to make up their own identity. If not Christianity, then other ideologies and philosophies will take control of the youth. What better ideology for them to follow then than the life-changing, meaning-bringing, love-infusing ideology of Jesus of Nazareth? Youth have the right to be introduced to Jesus just as they are daily introduced, via popular culture, to other less-inspiring figures and ideas. It remains that this 4–14 missiology needs to consider the implication of leading youth who are part of non-evangelical or non-Christian families to Christ, and then having them face rejection from their only life-support at this stage in life, their families. Is the church ready to become the new family of youth ostracized from their blood families because of their change of religious affiliation?

The author of this chapter's background section mentions the youth as part of God's mission. She also states that youth are challenging the church to move in new directions, and that indeed is a vital ingredient for Middle Eastern churches today. However, it seems that what she has in mind is youth as targets for the church's evangelism. She surveys the church's ministry among orphans, child evangelism, education initiatives and ecumenical work by youth leaders, and all that is commendable and praiseworthy. But can the youth be part of God's mission as participants in it and not only recipients of it? Perhaps Jesus's commandment for his disciples to pray for more workers for the harvest (Matt 9:38 and Luke 10:2) might find its answer in the youth of our day bursting with energy but also spending countless idle hours on social media and video games. In the Old Testament God chose a weak enslaved nation to covenant with and through whom he would bless other nations. Jesus was radical in choosing his co-workers and followers: he entrusted God's mission to fishermen, tax collectors and women; people who in his day were not considered worthy of religious work in any way. Does the church need to be more radical in choosing who goes about *doing* God's mission? Are the youth, children and teenagers of our day the un-thought of workers in the field waiting to be called by the church to action? I can say, with some conviction, give me one hundred youth who fear nothing but sin and desire nothing but God, more than video games and pornography, and they will set up the kingdom of heaven upon the earth![15]

Some churches, at least in Lebanon, do allow youth to participate in the church's mission. However, a troubling phenomenon is that they end up being part of "blue-collar" church work. More often than not you will find youth leading the games in the Sunday School programmes, flipping the slides of the worship lyrics, and perhaps – if they happen to be the pastor's child – collecting the offering on Sundays. That is commendable work and a step in the right direction. There is no hierarchy in God's eyes between the pastor preaching on Sunday and the young lady arranging the Bibles on Saturday. Moreover, allowing youth to participate in the church, even if in minute tasks, is better than having them completely alienated from any work. However, we seem to be, as churches and as a society, stuck in the disciples' cry against children to stay away from Jesus (Matt 19:14, Mark 10:14 and Luke 18:16). Are we failing to hear the rebuke of Jesus? How many youth preach on Sundays, lead discipleship groups, teach in Bible studies, sit on church committees, lead the worship, or have a say in the church's decision-making? Dare we begin to ask the same question of female youth? By keeping youth off the leadership of the church, are we losing a prophetic voice that could speak renewal into our society? Are perhaps our leaders burned out because they are refusing to dip into the untouched reservoir of energy, enthusiasm, faith, and talent that is the children and teenagers of our church and society?

---

15. A humble play on John Wesley's famous quote: "Give me one hundred men who fear nothing but sin . . ." Robert Campbell, "Ten Thought-Provoking John Wesley Quotes," 29 April 2011; https://blog.logos.com/2011/04/ten_thought-provoking_john_wesley_quotes/ (accessed 25 April 2018).

A pertinent observation to this discussion is the fact that some or most of the disciples of Jesus, the famous twelve, could have been teenagers under the age of eighteen. Otis and Frank Cary note that "painters have been inclined to represent most of the twelve disciples as heavily bearded men, apparently in middle life if not beyond it."[16] After a list of evidence, the authors conclude that a better picture of the disciples is that of "a band of [young] students eager to receive instruction from the wonderful teacher who has aroused their enthusiasm and won their hearts."[17] If Jesus chose to spend most of his time with youth, be they teenagers as argued above or young adults, and entrusted his Father's kingdom to a group of youth, how would that change the way we view youth in the church's mission? Cary and Cary present historical evidence that rather than only being likely, it is probable that those who bring Christianity to new places happen to be young. They cite the example of Japan where the earliest converts were students aged thirteen to nineteen who then went on, under severe persecution, to spread the gospel to others.[18]

In fact, the examples of Maher and Souhail similarly show how a young person's commitment to Christ burns strongly into their future and brings forth more enthusiasm for ministry. Interestingly for our discussion, the case study asserts that Souhail, after becoming a Christian, began to help in the youth ministry of his local church during his teenage years. However, the author does not explore this part of Souhail's life, but immediately jumps to his adult ministry among youth, a wonderful ministry which I have witnessed first-hand. Personally, just as I am interested in Souhail and Maher's adult ministry among youth and the creative models they are using to attract youth to Christ, I am also interested in their respective teenage years. Did they find it easy, especially for Maher and his traditional Christian background, to fit into a local evangelical congregation? Did they find room for ministry? How did that period form their later perspectives of, and practice in, ministry among youth?

As an active youth minister, I find it is rather easy to dazzle youth with sport programmes, fun camps, engaging talks and wonderful parties. However, I find it challenging to get them engaged with the local church. It is as if we have two churches. On the one hand there are the cool youth meetings with the games, talks, food, fellowship and "24-hours-without-sleep" YFC Christmas programme; children and teenagers flock to these events. On the other hand,

---

16. Otis Cary and Frank Cary, "How Old Were Christ's Disciples," *The Biblical World* 50, no. 1 (1917): 3.

17. Cary and Cary, "How Old," 11–12.

18. Cary and Cary, 7–8.

there is the "adult" church on Sunday with its six-verse hymns, archaic Arabic Bible readings and long sermons. Maher and Souhail made it into adult life as committed Christians and active ministers among the youth. What about the hundreds and thousands who attended the same outreaches as those two, who also gave their lives to Christ, and who also made decisions to follow Christ at the same age and in the same groups as Maher and Souhail? Where are they now? It would be of paramount importance to ask them, and others, what happened during their teenage years to keep them committed to the body of Christ. It would also be of paramount importance to ask the others, though that might well be impossible, what took them away from the body of Christ as they arrived in the world of adults.

Ministry among children and teenagers is important. They are the future of the church, and mission to them pushes the church to adopt innovative ways to share and live the gospel. However, as this reflection has shown, perhaps we are in need of a renewal of our minds on youth ministry. Youth are the future of the church, but also its present. Youth are the recipients of the church's mission, but also its practitioners. Youth, I humbly propose, need to become a full part of the church and all its ministries of teaching, evangelism, house visits, social work, education and others. As we of the adult world shed some of our power in an act of radical sharing with the least of these, children and teenagers, perhaps we shall see the kingdom of God break forth in a radical sharing of God's love for the world.

10

Leadership Formation in the Mission of God

Our final chapter focuses on the training of Christian leaders, both priests and pastors of churches as well as leaders of Christian organizations. It picks up from several challenges raised earlier. The increasing number of churches, be they formally recognized or otherwise, necessitates the emergence of more leaders, as was mentioned in chapter 1. The spread of work amongst specific age groups such as children and youth including through Katalyst as described in the previous chapter necessitates the training of all those with the required aptitude and sense of calling.

The material was written by members of faculty at ABTS, Lebanon. Our missiological reflection is by Walid Zailaa with preceding contributions by Rabih Hasbany and Chaden Hani (see contributors' bios).

Background: A Plethora of Seminaries (by Rabih Hasbany)

Middle Eastern Christians today have a responsibility to proclaim their faith in word and deed to a world of more than 313 million Arabic speakers.[1] For these Christians and their leaders to faithfully carry out their duty, they need adequate training. As a result, there exists a variety of seminaries, schools of theology, Bible schools and other education and training programmes available in the Middle East for students to acquire theological education and leadership formation. Needless to say, theology is not a new subject to the Middle East,

---

1. *Ethnologue: Languages of the World.* www.ethnologue.com/ (accessed 12 December 2018).

as the region has given birth throughout the years to many great theologians such as Athanasius the Great, Ephrem the Syrian, John of Damascus, Gregory of Narek and many others.[2] As it appears on the website of the Middle East Council of Churches (MECC),[3] almost all churches can be classified as belonging to one of four families, namely, The Oriental Orthodox churches, the Eastern Orthodox churches, the Catholic churches and the Protestant and evangelical churches. The numerous seminaries can be classified in the same way.

First, the Oriental Orthodox family of churches: the most important seminary of the Coptic Church of Alexandria is the Coptic Theological Seminary in Cairo. The original school was in Alexandria, but it was closed by the Byzantine emperor at the Council of Chalcedon. In 1893, the Theological College in Alexandria was re-established and today has branches in Cairo, Tanta, Shebeen, Port Said, Mahala and Luxor. It also has branches in Australia, the USA, the UK and Germany.

In 1930, Patriarch Sahak Khabaian founded a theological seminary of the Arminian Church in Bikfaya (Lebanon) as an extension of the one already existing in Cilicia.

The Saint Ephrem Faculty of Theology, a theological seminary of the Syrian Orthodox Church, was established in 1996 in Maarat, Sidnaya in Syria. Prior to its establishment in Syria, this seminary operated from several locations in Lebanon and Iraq.

Second, moving to the Eastern Orthodox family, the clergy of the Greek Orthodox Churches of Alexandria, Jerusalem and Cyprus study theology in the faculties in Athens and Thessaloniki. In addition, the School of Athanasius the Great in Alexandria provides courses in theology and other disciplines in order to prepare missionaries.

The clergy of the Orthodox Church of Antioch receive their educational training at the St John of Damascus Institute of Theology, a faculty of the University of Balamand and connected with the Balamand Monastery of Our Lady the Virgin Mary in north Lebanon.[4] In 1832, Archimandrite Athanasius Kasir of Damascus established the first clerical school at Balamand with a focus on teaching Arabic, ecclesiastical music, Greek, dogmatics and practical ethics. Although it closed in 1840, the school reopened after the election of

---

2. J. L. Elias, *A History of Christian Education: Protestant, Catholic and Orthodox Perspectives* (Malbar: Krieger, 2002), 34.

3. https://mecc.org/ (accessed 7 December 2018).

4. http://theology.balamand.edu.lb/index.php/about-us/history (accessed 12 December 2018).

Patriarch Malatius II Dumani who gave special attention to the school. In 1914 the school closed again during the First World War but resumed after the war ended. In 1962, the standard of education was improved to the level of the Lebanese Baccalaureate Part II. Today the Institute grants various degrees in theological studies and offers online courses in theology and biblical studies.

Third, Lebanon is home to the main centres of Catholic theological education. The Holy Spirit University of Kaslik includes the Pontifical Faculty of Theology.[5] The seeds of this faculty started with the efforts of the Lebanese Maronite Order in 1695. The Lebanese state acknowledged it as a faculty of theology in 1962. In 1974, it became the official faculty of the Catholic church in Lebanon under an official mandate of the Lebanese Assembly of Catholic Patriarchs and Bishops. This was ratified by Rome in 1982. The faculty prepares students by teaching them to think critically as they study theology in dialogue with other disciplines, especially philosophy and the humanities. The Catholic church recognizes the importance of theological training for the revival of pastoral ministry.

Founded in 1936 by the Society of Pauline Fathers, the Saint Paul Institute of Philosophy and Theology of the Melkite Church of Antioch is based in Harisa, Lebanon. The institute grants a Licence of Philosophy and a Licence in Theology.

Historically, Jesuits are key players in the development of Catholic theological education in Lebanon. In 1846, they founded a seminary in Ghazir, and in 1875 established St Joseph University in Beirut. The Faculty of Theology was founded in 1881 and has been functioning ever since.[6] The Faculty serves as an umbrella for four different institutions: The Faculty of Religious Sciences, the Higher Institute for Religious Sciences, the Institute of Islamo-Christian Studies, and the Center for Arab Christian Documentation and Research.

The Antonine University in Baabda, Lebanon was established in 1990 by the Antonine order.[7] Administered by the Antonine Fathers and monks, it offers courses in theological education to laypeople and members of monastic orders through its Faculty of Biblical, Ecumenical and Religious Studies and the Faculty of Theology and Pastoral Studies.

Sagesse University in Beirut has a Faculty of Canon Law that is affiliated with the Pontifical Lateran University in Rome. The Sagesse Superior Institute

---

5. www.usek.edu.lb/en/pontifical-faculty-of-theology/fpt-overview (accessed 12 December 2018).

6. www.usj.edu.lb/english/index_temp.php (accessed 12 December 2018).

7. www.ua.edu.lb/french/home (accessed 12 December 2018).

of Law was founded in 1875 and remains committed to the mission of the Catholic church.[8] The university has also a Faculty of Ecclesiastical Science that offers degrees in theology.

Egypt has two Catholic Institutions. The first is the Faculty of Human and Theological studies founded in 1879. In 1990, it was integrated with the Urbaniana University in Rome and became the pontifical university of the Catholic Church in Egypt. The second is the Faculty of Religious Sciences founded in 1978, which belongs to the Egyptian Assembly of Catholic Patriarchs and Bishops. The faculty offers theological education to clergy and laypeople coming from different Catholic denominations across Egypt and the region.

In October 1973, the Lasallian tradition founded the Bethlehem University. In 1998, the Department of Religious studies was inaugurated within the Faculty of Arts.[9] It trains catechists and offers Christian religious education to all students.

The Babel Faculty of Theology in Baghdad was founded by the Synod of the Chaldean church in 1991. The faculty works in cooperation with the Holy Spirit University of Kaslik.

Finally in our review we move to the evangelical and other Protestant churches. In 1863, Presbyterian missionaries to Egypt founded the Evangelical Theological Seminary in Cairo (ETSC).[10] It started as a floating campus on board the houseboat *Ibis*, as the missionaries sailed between Assyut and Cairo. The current building was established in 1926 in central Cairo, inaugurated by the Evangelical Synod of the Nile. A library was added in 1967 and student housing in 1994. In addition, an extension of ETSC in Alexandria was founded in 1986, an initiative of the Evangelical Synod of the Delta.

The Near East School of Theology (NEST) has been a key centre for evangelical theological studies in Lebanon.[11] It was formed in 1932 as a result of a merger of the School for Religious Workers in Beirut and the School of Religion in Athens after missionaries in the Middle East proposed to unite the theological schools of Athens and Beirut. After negotiations between what were then the Syria Mission and the Near East Mission, an agreement was reached to merge the two schools and form the Near East School of Theology in Beirut.

---

8. www.uls.edu.lb/faculty/canon-law (accessed 12 December 2018).

9. www.bethlehem.edu/about/mission-history (accessed 12 December 2018).

10. http://etsc.org/new/our-history (accessed 12 December 2018).

11. www.theonest.edu.lb/en/Home (accessed 12 December 2018).

In 1966, the Lebanese Ministry of Education officially recognized NEST as an Institution of Higher Learning.

The Arab Baptist Theological Seminary was founded in 1960 in Mansourieh, Beirut to serve the church in the MENA region.[12] Its roots as a Baptist institution go back to 1893, when a young Lebanese Baptist named Sa'eed Juriedini began ministry in the region. Over the years many Baptist churches, hospitals and schools were established in Lebanon and neighbouring countries. This created the need for a college to train church and other Christian leaders. In 1948, Finlay Graham, a missionary who had moved from Jordan to Beirut, started to provide such leadership formation. He and others wanted to establish a Baptist seminary and their efforts gave birth to ABTS with Finlay Graham as its first president. Since then ABTS has been equipping emerging leaders from multiple evangelical backgrounds and churches from different countries in the MENA region.

Among other evangelical institutions in Lebanon are the Eastern Mediterranean Nazarene Bible College, the Mediterranean Bible College (Church of God), the Christian Alliance Institute for Theology, and Lebanon Baptist Seminary in Ain Najm.

Jordan Evangelical Theological Seminary (JETS) was officially founded on 23 March 1995 in Amman.[13] Classes were conducted in various rented locations until JETS moved into its own campus in 2013. The founder, Dr Imad Shehadeh, continues to serve as president. JETS is committed to fulfilling its mission of equipping Arab leaders for the Middle East to the people living in the twenty-two countries of the Arabic speaking world.

Bethlehem Bible College (BBC) was founded in 1979, led by Bishara Awad who had returned to Palestine after studying in the United States.[14] He presented his idea to a group of Arab Orthodox, Catholic, Lutheran, Anglican and evangelical pastors. Hope Christian School offered its campus for BBC to begin evening classes with nine students. During its first few years courses were taught by foreign missionaries due to the lack of local theology professors. However, BBC's faculty now includes many Palestinian evangelical scholars.

Missions have played a vital role in the founding of theological seminaries and Bible schools in the region. Institutions from different faith backgrounds have been established with the same goal of training and forming Christian men and women to better serve their communities in the MENA region and

---

12. www.abtslebanon.org (accessed 12 December 2018).

13. www.jets.edu (accessed 12 December 2018).

14. https://bethbc.edu/ (accessed 12 December 2018).

beyond. The responsibility for Christian leadership formation is shared by all these institutions.

Case Studies: The Formation of New Leaders (by Walid Zailaa and Chaden Hani)

> *Our first case study is the story of the transformation of one man and the effects of that upon his family and others that he is associated with. It illustrates that leadership formation for some occurs in settings other than formal theological institutions.*
>
> *In contrast our second study looks at one institution, describing how its methods have changed to reflect that leadership requires more than academic theological knowledge.*

Fahd: A Man Transformed to Be a Christian Leader

Life shaped Fahd to be a street-smart man. He left Syria after the crisis erupted in 2011 (see appendix). He moved to Lebanon and found work in Beirut as a chef. Sometimes he was robbed of his salary, at other times he was dismissed because of his temper; both necessitated finding another restaurant that would employ him. Consequently, he experienced the life of a second-grade human being. He vainly tried to become acquainted with educated folks to gain some respect from those around him.

Fahd did not go to college, but he was smart, with a strong personality and an eagerness to learn. He had an interest in understanding God. Consequently, he read many philosophical and religious books and visited some religious leaders and non-Christian scholars to ask questions about their beliefs. After five years of searching for religious truth Fahd became a secularist.

Fahd is a married man with two children, and a member of an extended family which was dependent financially on him. However, his small family could not tolerate his nervous temper and his behaviour which made them decide not to come to Lebanon and live with him. When Fahd visited Syria to see his wife and children, as well as his extended family, he would come back after causing many conflicts.

We met Fahd when he visited our church. He first came by accident, brought by a mutual friend. Fahd was very critical of our faith since he is not from a Christian background, but in the church, he saw for the first time a group of people that shared the same beliefs and appeared to be content with each other. It seemed that the unity within the group was attractive to Fahd. The next week he did not come, but the following one he came and wanted to challenge our faith in Christ just to prove to himself and to the group that he was well informed. He sought to demonstrate his disapproval of all faiths since none had proved able to save the Middle East from conflict.

The pastor did not reject him; instead he offered him a simple explanation of the gospel of salvation through Christ. The congregation welcomed Fahd, and on his second visit they invited him to stay for dinner with a family. Week after week he came to the church meetings, and often had comments and questions that would challenge the pastor and other church leaders.

Everybody treated Fahd with grace despite his harsh comments and temper. He fought with almost everyone in church, but grace and prayer prevailed. After three months of constant attendance at our church meetings, Fahd prayed for the first time. It showed his inner struggle: the acceptance he received from the church community despite his behaviour towards them. He could not understand the reasons and motives these Christians had which were new to him since he had been expelled from every other group he had tried to belong to previously.

As time passed, Fahd started showing an interest in changing. He wanted to belong but felt that he needed to prove himself worthy of acceptance. He endeavoured to express his care about each and every member of the church community, big and small. He soon became the person everyone would call to help out when needed. He became engaged in visiting the members of the church and sought a family belonging he had missed.

After a further few months of regular commitment to the church life, including discussions and Bible studies, Fahd was able to apply biblical knowledge to his life and prayed for Jesus to help him overcome his inner challenges. Seeing his attempts and knowing his true intentions, the church and its members gave him some responsibilities. These tasks boosted his personality and helped him shape his leadership skills under the guidance and supervision of the church leaders.

The time came when Fahd had to go to Syria to visit his family. This visit was longer than usual. Upon his return he shared with the church the result of his changed behaviour on his six sisters and four brothers and the acceptance he had received from his wife and children. Another visit a few months later convinced some sisters to read the book that was responsible for the major change in their brother and made his wife decide to come and live with her husband in Lebanon.

At the time of writing Fahd lives in Lebanon with his contented family that comes to church every week, because only Jesus proved able to change the once intolerable man. His relationship with his wife has changed to become a relationship envied by all the extended family and community. Fahd, together with his wife and their two children, are now the family that their community highly respects, and Fahd has become the financial supporter of his extended family and a reference in all matters.

Affective, Behavioural and Cognitive Elements of Leadership

For more than fifty years, ABTS has been deeply involved in leadership formation in the MENA region. Over the years, ABTS's methods for training leaders have been gradually altered to reflect contemporary changes within local communities, thus ensuring that the leadership needs of the Arab church are met. As a result, ABTS's faculty adopted a different educational approach through which the "graduate profile" became the driving force to restructure the theology programme and core curriculum.

In the process, ABTS's faculty was keen to bring a holistic approach to the formation of potential leaders from the Arab world, looking to bring about progression at affective, behavioural and cognitive levels. Accordingly, faculty members have redesigned their units in the various modules, stating the various learning outcomes in their syllabi based on the aforementioned ABC – affective, behavioural and cognitive – learning outcomes.

ABTS's model of formation manifests itself in the variety of methods offered. The curriculum consists of formal and non-formal components through which the students are trained to think theologically in every aspect of their life and ministry.

The formal components of the curriculum are the accredited courses taught in the modules through four lenses: biblical-theological, historical-theological, sociological-cultural and personal-ministerial. Additionally, students are taught to bring the four lenses together in their integrative project toward the end of each module. The rationale of the integrative modules is a dialogue between the ABTS Vision focus on "God glorified, people reconciled, and communities restored" (God, individual, community) and the seven ABTS Foundational Values: namely, authentic worship, missional church, Christ-like leadership, empowerment, reflective practice, community cohesion, and personal and spiritual development.

The non-formal components of the curriculum are the accredited non-classroom learning activities. These include mentoring, discipleship groups, chapel, theological reflection on life and ministry, ministry practicum, induction, September diagnostics, capstone, and independent learning contracts. For credit to be granted the following three elements need to be in place: predetermined learning outcomes, predetermined learning tasks and activities with predetermined means of assessment. For this case study, I will look at the "theological reflection" as an example of non-formal credited components of the curriculum. ABTS exists for the purpose of "equipping faithful men and women for effective service."[15] For this to occur the learning that takes place in the classroom must be applied in the context of life and ministry. The process of theological reflection on life and ministry is a major component of a student's preparation for effective Christian leadership. In that all of life is a theological act, students are asked during the theological reflection component of the curriculum to reflect upon three things. First, various forms of ministry engagement. Second, elements of daily life such as family relationships, relationships with others in the ABTS community and on-campus employment. Third, current affairs in wider society. More advanced students are urged to engage in theological reflection on diverse issues. In all these exercises, students must keep in mind the end goal of their development as a leader who is able to interpret Christian life and ministry through the multiple lenses of Scripture, theology, history and community.

The most important characteristic that ABTS seeks in students is a commitment to grow as servant-leaders while they are with us – affectively, behaviourally and cognitively. We believe that if the students demonstrate a commitment to self-initiated holistic growth, they are more likely to continue this pattern after graduation. Consequently, the elements we seek to see in students as they move towards graduation include the following. First, a teachable spirit – not just in academic courses but also in personal and ministerial formation. Of particular concern is to see a teachable spirit, even where ABTS is not providing boundaries and direction.

Second, reducing levels of ABTS-initiated "maintenance." While some students may need substantial pastoral support at the beginning of their time with us, if this continues into the second and third years then we should question their long-term effectiveness as leaders.

Third, an increasingly positive influence on other students, particularly first-year students. We recognize that a growing relationship with God should be reflected in a growing positive influence on other students.

---

15. ABTS's Mission Statement, see https://abtslebanon.org/about/vision-mission/ (accessed 12 December 2018).

Fourth, self-initiated disciplines of growth, where students recognize an area of weakness and take positive steps to address it. We desire that the students are at the centre of the learning process, not ABTS or its faculty.

Missiological Reflection: from Reception to Responsibility (by Walid Zailaa)

In the beginning, the book of Genesis introduces YHWH as the God of Abraham to whom the promise to be God's representative was made. The mission of God started with Abraham and his descendants who, at one point in history, sought refuge in Egypt, escaping famine. The story unfolds by showing that through appointed leaders, such as the prophets, the priests, and sometimes the kings, God's plan was to organize the various aspects of the people's life so that he will be known to the nations as the true and living God of Israel. God's universal mission to the rest of the world was through the new role and identity he has bestowed on his people in Exodus: "you will be for me a kingdom of priests and a holy nation" (Exod 19:6).

However, Israel failed to fulfil its role as an agent of salvation to the world; nevertheless, God remained faithful to his covenant with Abraham. Despite the unfaithfulness of Israel in the Old Testament, God's universal plan to bring his mission to its completion and ultimate revelation has been successfully fulfilled in Jesus Christ. "Therefore, when the time had fully come, God sent his Son, born of a woman, born under law, to redeem those under law," as described by the apostle Paul in his epistle to the Galatians (Gal 4:4). With Jesus Christ, new elements have shaped the building blocks of "the people of God." It is not anymore from the exclusivity of Israel to the inclusivity of the nations. Rather, by faith in Jesus Christ the holistic and hybrid foundation of "the people of God" is forming the church.

In the last decade, thousands of books, lectures, seminars and webinars have discussed the meaning of the terms *leadership* and *mission*. It is nearly impossible to find one meaning that fits all. Nevertheless, almost everyone agrees that there is a common factor that holds the two terms in perspective and context. Our geographical location and the era we live in shape our understanding of leadership and mission. For years, in our Middle Eastern context, Christian leadership remained synonymous with "authority" and mission with "reception."

The notion of leadership has always been hierarchical and a top-down phenomenon in this part of the world. Leaders on the top of the hierarchy have the ultimate authority to the extent that it frequently becomes a vital part of their identity. They are so much engrained in their positions that most of the time they overlook potential and capable leaders in their midst, no matter how much their institution is suffering due to their age or unengaged leadership style. Unfortunately, the list of pastors and church leaders who have reached the age of retirement without training successors is long; as a result, the church is paying a high price. For that reason, at least in Lebanon, we started experiencing many churches that were devoid of pastors or leaders.

Like the concept of leadership, the notion of mission is also misinterpreted in this part of the world. In the Middle East, the feeling of inferiority and low self-esteem due to several factors, including Western stereotyping, has cornered us in the "reception" mindset when it comes to mission. From the dawn of missional history, we needed Western missionaries to establish and run schools, seminaries, hospitals and churches in the Arab world. No doubt, Western initiatives are based on a unique calling to obey the Lord in reaching out to us and for that we are thankful. Furthermore, much of what has been established in previous generations remains operational and effective. On the downside, however, this has left a scar in our understanding of mission. For too long, we have linked mission with incoming missionaries and with receiving financial resources, food-aid, medical supplies, educational material or any commodity that might be available for us. We had equated mission with reception and failed to learn the principle of giving or sending as we are given.

Although the Bible presents the concept of mission in the act of sending, and the model of leadership in the most glorious act of self-giving, we have always walked in the opposite direction. The fear of an identity crisis when we pave the way for others to take up the lead and the fear of losing our resources when we start reaching out has been embedded in the fabric of our Christian communities. Nevertheless, this bleak outlook in the Middle Eastern context has seen the light at the end of the tunnel. It is in the midst of suffering that the beacon of hope is shining again. When missionaries are persecuted, expelled and no longer can get into our countries, we have had to learn to be missionaries to our people. When the Western economy is hurt and no longer can provide, we have to learn to support others and ourselves. It is in the middle of chaos we get up, roll up and take up: we get up off our seats, roll up our sleeves and take up our responsibilities. A new Middle East is emerging and with it, our understanding of mission and leadership is being dramatically re-shaped.

The political and economic instability in most Middle Eastern countries, the ugliness of the war in Syria (see appendix) and the rise of militant movements have shaped the whole area. The new Middle East I am referring to is not born out of post-modernity and scientific advancement for the common good of humanity; rather is born out the ashes of its sons and daughters. The new Middle East is being forged in the furnace of oppression, pain and suffering. As a result, the recent demographical changes that the whole area is witnessing due to internal displacement and migration have created an urgent need for a new mindset. The church is facing systematic persecution in most of the North African countries as well as Egypt and Sudan, is standing fast in war zones in Syria and Iraq, and is straining under the heavy burden of refugees in Lebanon and Jordan. In times of crisis, leading from the ivory tower is no longer a valid definition of "leadership" in the dictionary of the contemporary Middle East. Similarly, the notion of "mission" is not to be deemed as a foreign hand reached out to us, rather our hands stretched out to help our people. After all, is it not a biblical mandate for each one of us to be a missionary and a servant leader? I wonder if we need such times to be reminded of this biblical truth.

The ABTS is one of many institutions, such as ETSC in Egypt, JETS in Jordan, NEST in Lebanon and BBC in Bethlehem, that has shaped its vision around the leadership formation of its students to be missionaries in their churches, communities and the Arab world. For that reason, equipping faithful men and women for ministry in the Middle East and North Africa has been the mission of the seminary for more than a decade. The longer and harsher the crisis is, the stronger the church becomes in its quest to train potential leaders for ministry. Furthermore, ABTS has developed an ambitious plan to equip local faculty and scholars, who can teach theology and write academically, for its own ministry in theological education in service of the church. Needless to say, the aforementioned seminaries work together to support the local church in its mission. I am looking at the leadership formation from my standpoint as an evangelical serving at ABTS. My perspective is, therefore, limited to the ministry of ABTS and does not cover the broader evangelical community in detail nor the ministry of other Christian denominations, many of which are missional and are deeply rooted in the Middle East, as described in the background section of this chapter.

Many spectators, locally and internationally, are looking at the current crisis cynically, concluding that Christianity in the Middle East is on the verge of extinction. In spite of their analytical and critical perception, they are investigating the present circumstances without considering the Christian aspects of the Middle East's history during the past two thousand years. Additionally, they are scratching the surface without looking deeply at the number of those who are getting to know Jesus Christ and believe in him having been raised as adherents of another religion. Fahd in the first case study is a great example of someone who came to faith as a result of being displaced from Syria. It was nearly impossible to reach people like him in their hometown with the message of the gospel. Despite the bitterness of the war in the Middle East, the church in Lebanon and elsewhere is serving thousands of displaced persons. Despite the systematic persecution in North Africa, the church is witnessing thousands of people coming to faith. God is working through his church in the MENA region. Like Esther in the Old Testament, God has preserved the church for such times (Esth 4:14b). The church is the beacon of hope that will eventually explode and shine all over the place. It is through those who believed in the mission of God through the church that leadership formation would take place. Working alongside the church is the hope we have left for a better tomorrow.

The mission of God behind the biblical story has been always initiated through the leadership formation of potential individuals. The mission of God in the Old Testament started with individuals like Abraham, Isaac, Jacob, Moses, Joshua, David and others, all of whom God had shaped, including their leadership skills, for a greater mission to many nations. Similarly, the New Testament teaches us how Jesus appointed his disciples and trained them to lead the church toward a greater mission to the end of the earth, starting from Jerusalem, Judea and Samaria (e.g. Acts 1:8). The story of the Bible is our story. As Jesus commissioned his disciples, he is commissioning his church today. Leadership formation in the church is a key factor for a successful missional journey in obedience to the Lord's commandment in the MENA region and beyond.

Conclusion

Mission in the Middle East is diverse, complex and adaptable. The local context profoundly shapes how the church conducts itself within the societies of which it is a long-standing and integral feature. We have seen how Jesus is the archetype of both proclamation and social justice.

The church has greater freedom in some parts than in others: some can overtly share the good news, others are obliged to be more discreet. Major events in the region and beyond during this century have created new opportunities for sharing the good news of Jesus at a time when there is more openness among non-Christians to exploring who Jesus is. More people throughout the Arab world are able to respond to the question that Jesus asked his first disciples: "'But what about you?' he asked. 'Who do you say I am?'" (Matt 16:15; Mark 8:29; Luke 9:20)

Much happens in small groups; other contact happens online. The results do not always look like traditional Christianity, including the evangelical variety. God is doing a new thing with some: we might say that some new wine is going in new wineskins (Matt 9:17).

Compassion ministries to meet human need are an essential element of *missio Dei*, of expressing who Jesus is: he is concerned for all. Social justice and the pursuit of peace are likewise essential elements of *missio Dei*. Likewise, Jesus's teaching about himself, the kingdom of God and the nature and character of the triune God must be made available to all who wish to explore it.

Discipleship is an ongoing, lifelong feature of Christians' daily lives. We noted that discipleship is innately relational, just as following Jesus is a relationship with him and that the very essence of God is relational: Father, Son and Spirit are one, indivisible Godhead.

We pointed out that evangelism and initial discipleship for new adherents of Christianity intertwine in various ways. For example, some materials first written for one are used by some for the other.

All of Christ's followers are members of his one, universal, catholic and apostolic church. Many are members of local churches in specific locations. Recognized places of Christian worship, church buildings, have been an integral part of the Middle East for generations. These facilities are significant to many Christians, an expression of belonging to a particular place. For some, the actual architecture of the building has theological significance. For others, particularly those from non-Christian backgrounds, access to a recognized church is problematic, even impossible. What happens for these Christians is very dependent on their local context. Some choose not to use the term Christian, simply identifying with Jesus. Typically, they meet in house fellowships, local churches whose structure is heavily influenced by their local context. As the number of such followers of Jesus rises, so the nature and expression of the church changes.

This affects how leaders are trained, whether to pastor churches, to serve as youth workers or to lead other Christian organizations. The church, God's people, is multi-generational. We have noted the call for children and youth to be treated as active participants in the church of today. It is in working with youth inside and beyond the church that future leaders can and are shaped. This affects *missio Dei* and has wider implications for societies and nations throughout the Arab world.

We have read an impassioned plea to use modern technology wisely and creatively, to make the good news available to the whole region and in carefully constructive ways designed to be accessible to specific groups within society. The opportunities are there to spread the good news in word as well as by deeds.

We need to be imaginative storytellers since the gospel of Jesus is the best story of all time.

We have acknowledged too that new technology brings new dangers. We need to assist one another in being wise in how we operate online and how we communicate about what God is doing. It is right to rejoice in God's kingdom growing before our eyes, yet our very rejoicing must not endanger that which we celebrate.

A related struggle is over who has control of resources and content. Who knows best how to reach particular communities? Often, it is the indigenous, here meant in a very specific sense. Some ministries in the Middle East are increasingly facilitating those of Muslim background to communicate about Jesus to their contemporaries.

We have noted the intrinsic role of interfaith dialogue in some places in the Middle East. Where it is absent, all-too-often strife and conflict ensue. So, the establishing and maintenance of firm relationships with those of other faiths is one arena in which Middle Eastern Christians are taking the lead, especially within evangelical Christianity. We observed that there can be no true witness to those of other faiths without dialogue and nor can there be authentic dialogue without witness.

Related to this is that working for peaceful, healthy societies is an expression of *missio Dei*. Typically, this requires working with people of goodwill from other faith backgrounds who share the same desire. It is essential to keep in mind that there is a human being in every person we encounter.

Several contributors have alluded to persecution, meaning religious motivated abuse, harassment or overt violation of recognized rights of an individual or group simply for loyalty to Jesus. Pressures on some Christians are intense, as alluded to in several case studies. Consequently, we must all be vigilant, ensuring that all we do and say about the church throughout the Arab world is supportive of it, and not in some ways making life more difficult for Christians in the region. Examples of this include having good online security and being careful about how we rejoice over more people choosing to become disciples of Jesus.

We noticed too the temptation facing some Christians and church leaders to accept an implicit agreement with autocratic political rulers that Christians will remain in Christian communities and inside church buildings in return for some degree of protection and acceptance. One contributor gave an overt challenge to this thinking. Whilst acknowledging the history and continuing pressures underlying such thinking, he noted that such agreements are not compatible with our primary identity as children of God and citizens of heaven. Jesus expects that all his followers will participate in *missio Dei*, expressing good news and performing acts of compassion to whoever they meet.

Above all, we have noticed how God continues to be at work. He is building his church. He is inspiring many to be participants with him in *missio Dei*. The forms this takes have changed over time and will no doubt continue to do so. These are exciting days in the Middle East and wider Arab world for those that look to see what God is doing.

Appendix

The Middle East from Christ to The Twenty-First Century – A Brief History

Many chapters refer to historical events in the Middle East during the twentieth and twenty-first centuries. The intention here is to put these into context, thereby describing the environment within which the church throughout the Middle East lives and expresses Christ. These events have shaped the peoples of the Middle East. What follows is a succinct summary of events; more detailed accounts of specific eras, countries and events have been provided by others.

Lest we forget, the church was founded in the Middle East, in Jerusalem on the first Pentecost shortly after the death, resurrection and ascension of Jesus. Arabs were present that day (Acts 2:9–11). The church in Egypt regards St Mark, the author of the Gospel with that name, as its founding father. In the first century the region was part of the Roman Empire. In the following centuries it was part of numerous empires, culminating in that of the Ottomans.

During the nineteenth century parts of the Ottoman Empire secured independence or became part of Western colonial systems. This included North Africa and Egypt. The remainder of the empire collapsed during the First World War (1914–1918). The Middle East came under colonial rule, mainly by the UK and France. The modern state of Turkey was inaugurated in 1923.

Many Middle Eastern countries gained their independence in the following period: Iraq in 1932, Lebanon in 1943, followed by Jordan and Syria in 1946.[1]

---

1. Jordan had a greater degree of autonomy during the British mandate period than most other areas of the Middle East.

The national borders were designated by the colonial powers. In the Middle East, the existence of nation states is a twentieth century development.

The exception to this general pattern was the area of Palestine. The UK handed control to the UN, whose Partition Plan of 1947 was formally accepted by representatives of the Jewish communities but rejected by the Palestinians. Conflict ensued, leading to the establishment of the state of Israel on 15 May 1948. Conflict persisted until 1949 when the division of the area into Israel, the West Bank and the Gaza Strip was internationally recognized. This situation changed with the Six Day War of June 1967 during which Israel took control of the Gaza Strip, West Bank including East Jerusalem, much of the Golan Heights and the Sinai Peninsula.

In the decades after the Second World War several Middle Eastern countries endured internal conflict. Egypt had a coup in 1952 in which King Farouk was removed from power and a President installed. The first three, Gamal Abdel-Nasser, Anwar Sadat and Hosni Mubarak were all formerly senior generals. During 1956 the UK and France assaulted Egypt, ostensibly over control of the Suez Canal. In the West, this event is known as the Suez Crisis. The US declined to support its European allies, obliging them to end their action and acknowledge Egyptian control of the canal.

There were numerous coups in Syria, including three in 1949 alone, before Hafez Assad came to power in 1969. He brought stability and continuity, albeit with a style of governance that severely repressed any criticism of his rule. Likewise, Iraq had a coup in July 1958 which replaced its colonial-installed monarchy with a presidential system which came to be dominated by Saddam Hussein from 1979.

In contrast, Jordan proved stable and the monarchy under the Hashemites has endured to this day. It was affected by the arrival of displaced Palestinians in the 1940s, many of whom were given citizenship and became integrated. A second wave in 1967 was treated differently. When dissent arose in 1970, Jordan acted decisively to quell protests and pushed many Palestinians out of the country. Some became settled in Syria, albeit with no citizenship and limited rights, whilst many migrated into Lebanon.

Lebanon's history has taken a different course. It was a mosaic of ethnic and religious groups from its founding. It endured an intense civil war which is typically dated as 1975 to 1991. There had been skirmishes in 1974. The conflict saw at least forty different Lebanese armed groups competing for control. In addition, there was involvement by Syria, Israel and a number of countries from outside the region. The Taif Accord of 1989 created a political framework for resolving the conflict. Syria assumed a large role within Lebanon, and

Israel maintained a presence in the south. The latter ended in 2000, whilst Syria's overt presence was withdrawn in 2005 in what became known as the Cedar Revolution. Lebanon has endured several bouts of conflict with Israel, notably in summer 2006, a conflict often referred to in the West as the Israel-Hezbollah war.

Another Arab country to experience a civil war was Algeria during the 1990s. These troubles displaced many people.[2] They also left a legacy of armed groups who have merged, split and changed names several times. Some have pledged allegiance to al-Qaeda and similar networks. This pattern has also occurred in Iraq, Syria and Yemen.

Several major events have reshaped the region. We will briefly consider three, the last of which continues to unfold.

First, in August 1990 Iraq invaded Kuwait. An international coalition including numerous Arab countries was assembled to reverse this situation, an event often referred to in the West as the Gulf War.[3] In February 1991 several Arab countries made international news television channels available via terrestrial broadcasting. They did so because everyone knew that state news broadcasts were heavily censored and therefore not trusted. One consequence was that people across the region became aware that uncensored news reporting was available to those with a satellite dish. The popularity of such equipment expanded rapidly. This new window on the world opened many people across the region to new ideas and sources of information and entertainment. The inauguration of Christian satellite television was motivated by these opportunities (see chapter 8).

Second, the events of 11 September 2001 (9–11) when commercial aircraft were hijacked and crashed into the World Trade Center in New York, the Pentagon in Washington DC, and a field in Pennsylvania proved significant across the MENA region. The fact that the perpetrators were Arabs prompted many throughout the region to start asking questions about the nature of Islam.

---

2. Estimates range from 500,000 to 1,500,000 for the peak number of internally displaced people which was in 1992. The upper figure is 4 to 5 percent of the population. Most relocated to the outskirts of large urban areas, creating slum areas with high unemployment, poverty and some malnutrition. The government continues to strive to respond adequately. It is understood that many have been able to return, although no survey has been undertaken in recent years.

3. In the region, the term Gulf War can be a reference to the Iran-Iraq War, 1980–1988, with the 1991 Iraq versus an international coalition war referred to as the Second Gulf War. Similar terms are sometimes applied to the US-led invasion of Iraq in 2003.

Third, the Arab Spring became prominent in 2011, having begun in late 2010 in Tunisia.[4] Mass protests in many countries called for greater dignity, more and better jobs, and some say in the governance structures. The practical results varied widely within Arab countries. Some saw the demise of long-standing rulers, including Tunisia (January 2011), Egypt (25 January 2011) and Libya (20 October 2011). Several countries negotiated these developments with careful management by the rulers and modest changes to laws and policies. Examples include Jordan and Morocco. In Syria, what emerged was a long-running conflict involving numerous local groups and a wide range of international actors supporting and equipping different factions. Many Syrian Christians have asked me not to describe this as a "civil war" since there are far too many foreign players involved for that to be an accurate description.

Egypt had a second revolution in 2013 when mass protests involving an estimated one third of the population led to the removal of then President Morsi. The senior military council, led by General Abdul Fattah al-Sisi, assumed control of the executive branch of government until a presidential election was held in 2015. Al-Sisi stepped down as general in order to be a candidate and was duly elected, a development that continued the pattern of Egyptian presidents being former generals.

Widespread protests had occurred in parts of the Middle East prior to 2011. In 2005, mass protests in Lebanon prompted the withdrawal of Syria's overt military and security forces. Arguably, a strong element of Syrian influence continued. Two earlier examples occurred within the Israel-Palestine context known as intifadas (literally, uprisings). The first is usually dated 1987 to 1992 and was a contributory factor to the talks that produced the Oslo Accords of 1993. The second began in September 2000 and is widely regarded as ending in 2003. During both, violent means were employed by some amidst the peaceful protests and civil disobedience of many.

The aspirations of the Arab Spring remain largely unfulfilled. Significantly, many within the younger generations throughout the Middle East desire change.

Within the narrative of political changes since the First World War there have also been significant changes concerning religious matters. We need to highlight one change affecting Muslims before focusing on Christians.

---

4. Other titles are used by some commentators, including Arab Awakening and Arab Revolutions. See for example Andrews, *Identity Crisis*, 120–135.

For Islam, one key change was the ending of the Caliphate in 1924.[5] Prior to this, the Sultan (ruler) of the Ottoman Empire also held the title of Caliph, leader of Muslims. In practice, this was limited to Sunnis. The emerging new nation state of Turkey adopted a secular nature under its founder Kamal Ataturk. Consequently, the term Caliph was dropped. In practice, al Azhar university in Egypt became the highest-ranking religious authority in Sunni Islam, at least from a theological viewpoint. This separated religious and political authority.

Within Christianity, a general pattern emerged affecting churches. Most senior church leaders formed a relationship with their political rulers, effectively accepting protection and freedom for Christian worship in church buildings with restrictions on political engagement and critique of political matters. In this arrangement, church leaders maintained their pastoral responsibilities for Christian people but surrendered the prophetic voice. This arrangement came under pressure with the advent of the Arab Spring: should church leaders support the protests or the rulers? There continues to be no easy answer to this dilemma. Yet, many young Christians are profoundly disturbed that their religious leaders are supportive of political institutions that have failed to provide the dignity and jobs that their generation craves.

Conversely, the Arab Spring has changed the role of the church within society, at least in some parts of the Middle East. For example, Ramez Atallah has observed that "the church became an integral part of Egyptian society in ways that we could not have envisaged."[6]

5. See for example, Lausanne Global Analysis, *What Is the Islamic Caliphate and Why Should Christians Care?* May 2017; accessed 4 December 2018; www.lausanne.org/content/lga/2017-05/islamic-caliphate-christians-care.

6. Ramez Atallah, "Reflections on the Christians of Egypt Today," in *The Church in Disorienting Times*, ed. Jonathan Andrews (Carlisle: Langham Global Library, 2018), 13.

Glossary

4–14 Window: The age-range four to fourteen inclusive.

10/40 Window: The area of the world between ten and forty degrees north from the Atlantic to the Pacific oceans in which most of the least-reached people groups (see below) are located; the concept was developed by mission strategists in the West.

Alawites: An ethnic religious group with significant communities in Lebanon, Syria and Turkey; the religious aspect is regarded by some as part of Shi'a Islam and by others as a distinct religion outside of Islam.

Al Bustani: See Van Dyck

Amazigh: An ethnic group present in Morocco; one of the Berber (see below) tribes.

Arab Spring: A socio-political phenomenon that arose in 2011 affecting most countries in the Middle East, North Africa and the Arabian Peninsula typified by protests calling for reform of governance structures, greater opportunity for all and recognition of the dignity and worth of all citizens; referred to as the Arab Awakening and Arab Revolutions by some.

Arab world: Those countries located in the Middle East, North Africa and the Arabian Peninsula where Arabic is a national language (and the mother tongue of many citizens); namely Algeria, Bahrain, Egypt, Iraq, Jordan, Kuwait, Lebanon, Libya, Mauritania, Morocco, Oman, Qatar, Palestine, Saudi Arabia, Sudan, Syria, Tunisia, United Arab Emirates (UAE) and Yemen; many citizens of these countries are not ethnically Arab, e.g. the Kurds, Druze and the various Berber (see below) peoples across North Africa; the term "Arab world" can suggest a uniformity when the reality is diversity amongst these 19 states.

Armenian genocide: Term used to describe events in 1914 and 1915 in which many Armenian people were murdered, forcibly displaced or died while fleeing from the Ottoman authorities; Turkey rejects use of the word genocide for these events.[1]

---

1. See for example Andrews, *Last Resort*, 58–61.

Berber: A collective term for the indigenous peoples of North Africa who predate the arrival of Arabs during the expansion of the Arab empire in the seventh century.

Capuchins: A monastic order within the Roman Catholic church, closely aligned with St Francis of Assisi.[2]

Dom: An ethnic group present in Iraq, Israel-Palestine, Jordan, Lebanon, Syria and Turkey; typically, impoverished and marginalized; many resident in Lebanon were given nationality during the 1990s; referred to as gypsies or Nawars in some sources; many speak Domari as well as the local language; originate in northern India but have been present in the Middle East for many generations.

Dominicans: A monastic order with Roman Catholicism.

Druze: An ethnic and religious group found in Lebanon, Syria and Israel; the religious element is regarded as part of Islam by some; operates like a secret society with induction in successive levels.

iconostasis: A wall of icons and religious paintings separating the nave and sanctuary in Eastern Orthodox churches; can also refer to a movable stand of icons that can be placed anywhere within a church building.

identificational repentance: An act of apology or repentance made on behalf of others, often ancestors or a nation state; the person doing so is not accepting personal responsibility for wrongful acts committed by others. They are acknowledging that injury has occurred.

ISIS: An armed group that arose in Iraq around 2006 before re-emerging in Syria in late 2011 or 2012; the group's original official title was The Islamic State of Iraq and ash-Sham; it is referred to as The Islamic State in Iraq and Syria (ISIS) and The Islamic State in Iraq and the Levant (ISIL) in some sources because the Arabic phrase Belad As-Sham can refer to Syria and also the entire Levant (see below); the group re-titled itself The Islamic State in July 2014; the term Daesh (derived from an approximate acronym of the group's name in Arabic) is used by some in the Middle East.

Jesuits: A branch of Catholic Christianity.

---

2. See www.capuchin.com/ (accessed 12 December 2018).

Jesus Film: A film about the life of Jesus based on Luke's Gospel; it has been translated into numerous languages (www.jesusfilm.org).

Kabyle: An ethnic group in Algeria; one of the many tribes comprising the Berbers, the inhabitants of North Africa prior to the arrival of Arabs during the seventh century.

kafala: System used in some countries under which employers sponsor the residency permits of their staff; one effect is to tie the employee to the one employer, which reduces the rights of the employee; it often makes challenging poor working conditions and treatment problematic.

Levant: Literally, the lands around Damascus; typically understood to mean modern-day Iraq, Jordan, Lebanon and Syria; some usages include Israel, the West Bank and the Gaza Strip.

Messianic Jews: Ethnically Jewish people who accept and follow Jesus Christ as the Messiah.

millenarianism: Belief by a social, political or religious group in a coming major transformation after which all things will be changed; change may occur due to a cataclysmic event; within Christianity, a part of eschatology with several variations.

millet: A recognized religious order with authority from the state to operate a court system covering personal status law such as marriage, divorce, custody of children, burial rites and inheritance.

minoritization: The overt suppression of one group by another, usually (but not always) the larger suppressing the smaller.[3]

Monophysite: A branch within Christianity, also referred to as the Oriental Orthodox churches; this strand emerged following the Council of Chalcedon held in 451 when some Christians rejected the council's consensus on a certain Christological definition of the relationship between the two natures of Jesus Christ, i.e. fully divine and fully human.

Nestorian: A branch within Christianity; historically, it emerged following the Council of Ephesus held in 431 at which the Christological ideas ascribed to

---

3. See Martin Accad, "From Minority Status to the Fateful Embrace of Minoritization" in Jonathan Andrews, ed., *The Church in Disorienting Times* (Carlisle: Langham Global Library, 2018), 87–97.

Nestorius were condemned; however, the split was more for political reasons, with theological matters used for public relations purposes. (It is debatable whether Nestorius was a Nestorian. The views of many active theologians at this time are only known through their opponents, who were not necessarily the most accurate or generous in their assessments.)

Ottoman Empire: An empire ruled by the Ottoman Turks with its capital in Istanbul; it collapsed during World War One, being replaced by the nation state of Turkey with other territories having gained independence or coming under colonial mandates.

people group: A homogenous group of people, linguistically, culturally and religiously, and often also nationally; arose from the Homogenous Unit Principle, the view that church growth is most rapid in monocultural settings; so people groups arose to identify homogenous units; in turn, this led to the term Unreached People Groups (UPG) meaning a people group with no identifiable church or Christian presence, and then to Unengaged and Unreached People Groups (UUPG) meaning a UPG with no known missional presence; these terms were devised by mission strategists in the West.

Rum Orthodox: The Greek Orthodox Church which uses Arabic as its linguistic medium.

Shi'a: A major strand within Islam; the adjective form is Shi'ite.

soteriology: The study of the theology of salvation, a branch of theology.

Sunni: A major strand within Islam; numerically, the largest such strand.

Van Dyck: A well-known and long-standing translation of the Bible into Arabic; sometimes referred to as the al Bustani version after the primary translator.

Bibliography

Abu-Nimer, Mohammad, and Amal I. Khoury, and Emily Welty. *Unity in Diversity: Interfaith Dialogue in the Middle East.* Washington DC: United States Institute of Peace, 2007.

Accad, Fouad. *Building Bridges: Christianity and Islam.* Colorado Springs: Navpress, 1997.

———. "The Qur'an: A Bridge to Christian Faith." *Missiology: An International Review,* July 1976.

Accad, Martin. "Christian Attitudes towards Islam and Muslims: A Kerygmatic Approach." In *Toward a Respectful Understanding & Witness Among Muslims.* Edited by Evelyne A. Reisacher. Pasadena: William Carey Library, 2012.

Andrews, Jonathan, ed. *The Church in Disorienting Times: Leading Prophetically through Adversity.* Carlisle: Langham Publishing, 2018.

———. *Identity Crisis: Religious Registration in the Middle East.* Malton: Gilead Books, 2016.

———. *Last Resort: Migration and the Middle East.* Malton: Gilead Books, 2017.

Azumah, John. "Evangelical Christian Views and Attitudes towards Christian-Muslim Dialogue." *Transformation* 29, no. 2 (2012): 128–138.

Badr, Habib, ed. *Christianity: A History in the Middle East.* Beirut: MECC, 2005.

———. "Evangelical Churches and Missions in the Middle East." In *Christianity: A History in the Middle East.* Edited by Habib Badr. Beirut: MECC, 2005.

———. "The Protestant Evangelical Community in the Middle East: Impact on Cultural and Societal Developments." *International Review of Mission* 89, no. 352 (Jan 2000): 60–69.

Barnett, Jens. "Narrative, Identity and Discipleship." *Musafir: A Bulletin of Intercultural Studies* 3, no. 2 (December 2009): 3–5.

Barth, Karl. *Church Dogmatics: The Doctrine of the Word of God,* vol. 1, 2. Translated by H. Knight and G. T. Thomson. Edinburgh: T&T Clark, 1956.

———. *The Call to Discipleship.* Minnesota: Fortress Press, 2003.

Berkhof, Louis. *Systematic Theology.* Grand Rapid: Eerdmans, 1959.

Bonhoeffer, Dietrich. *The Cost of Discipleship.* Danvers: SCM Press, 1959.

———. *No Rusty Swords: Letters, Lectures and Notes from the Collected Works of Dietrich Bonhoeffer,* edited by Edwin H. Robertson and John Bowden. London: Collins, 1970.

Bosch, David J. "Evangelism: Theological Currents and Cross-Currents Today." *International Bulletin of Missionary Research* 11, no. 3 (1987): 98–103.

Brewster, Dan, and John Baxter-Brown, ed. *Children and Youth as Partners in Mission.* Compassion International, 2013.

Brueggemann, Walter. *The Prophetic Imagination,* 2nd edition. Minneapolis: Fortress Press, 2001.

Cary, Otis, and Frank Cary. "How Old Were Christ's Disciples?" *The Biblical World* 50, no. 1 (1917): 3–12.

Chapman, Colin. *Whose Promised Land? The Continuing Crisis over Israel and Palestine.* 3rd ed. Oxford: Lion Hudson, 2015.

Das, Rupen, and Julie Davidson. *Profiles of Poverty: The Human Face of Poverty in Lebanon.* Beirut: Dar Manhal al Hayat, 2011.

Donohue, John J. *Muslim-Christian Relations: Dialogue in Lebanon.* Occasional Papers Series. Washington, DC: Center for Muslim-Christian Understanding, History and International Affairs. Georgetown University, 1996.

Durkheim, Émile. *The Elementary Forms of Religious Life.* New York: Free Press, 1995.

Elias, J. L. *A History of Christian Education: Protestant, Catholic and Orthodox Perspectives.* Malbar: Krieger Publishing, 2002.

Erickson, Millard J. *Christian Theology.* Grand Rapids: Baker Books, 2002.

Farhadian, Charles E. *Introducing World Christianity.* Oxford: Blackwell Publishers, 2012.

Garrison, David. *A Wind in the House of Islam: How God Is Drawing Muslims around the World to Faith in Jesus Christ.* Monument: WIGTake Resources, 2014.

George, Sam, and Miriam Adenay, eds. *Refugee Diasporas: Missions amid the Greatest Humanitarian Crisis of Our Times.* Pasadena: William Carey Publishing, 2018.

Global Connections. *Disciple Making Movements (DMM),* 17 February 2017. Accessed 29 October 2018; www.globalconnections.org.uk/sites/newgc.localhost/files/papers/2017_dmm_-_towards_best_practices.pdf.

Gopin, Marc. *Holy War, Holy Peace: How Religion Can Bring Peace to the Middle East.* New York: Oxford University Press, 2002.

Groody, Daniel G. *Globalization, Spirituality, and Justice: Navigating the Path to Peace, Theology in Global Context.* Maryknoll: Orbis Books, 2007.

Hirvonen, Heidi. *Christian-Muslim Dialogue: Perspectives of Four Lebanese Thinkers.* Leiden, Netherlands: Koninklijke Brill NV, 2013.

Houssney, Georges. *Engaging Islam.* Treeline Publishing, 2010.

Huntington, Samuel. *The Clash of Civilizations and the Remaking of World Order.* New York: Touchstone, 1996.

Joseph, Suad. "The Future Today: Youth and Adolescents of the Middle East and North Africa." *Youth in the Arab World* (Nov 2011). Online. https://website.aub.edu.lb/ifi/public_policy/arab_youth/Documents/20111118ifi_unicef_youth_report/background_papers_series/20111103ifi_ay_unicef_background_paper_suad_joseph.pdf.

Kashouh, Hikmat. *Following Jesus in Turbulent Times.* Carlisle: Langham Global Library, 2018.

Kassir, Samir. *Beirut.* London: University of California Press, 2010.

Katanacho, Yohanna. *The Land of Christ.* Nazareth: self-published, 2012.

Kennedy, John W. "The 4–14 Window: New Push on Child Evangelism Targets the Crucial Early Years." *Christianity Today* 48, no. 7 (July 2004).

Kirk, J. Andrew. *The Church & The World: Understanding the Relevance of Mission.* Milton Keynes: Paternoster, 2014.

———. *What Is Mission? Theological Explorations.* Minneapolis: Fortress Press, 2000.

Ladd, George Eldon. *A Theology of The New Testament.* Grand Rapids: Eerdmans, 1993.

Laithy, H., K. Abu-Ismail, and K. Hamdan. *Country Study: Poverty, Growth and Income Distribution in Lebanon.* Brasilia: International Poverty Center, UNDP, 2008.

LaTourette, Kenneth Scott. *A History of Christianity: Reformation to the Present,* vol. 2. Peabody: Prince Press, 2003.

Mackay, John. *A Mentor Commentary: Exodus.* Fearn, Ross-shire: Christian Focus Publications, 2001.

Mathis, David. "Introduction." *Finish the Mission: Bringing the Gospel to the Unreached and Unengaged.* Edited by John Piper and David Mathis, 13–28. Wheaton: Crossway, 2012.

Moltmann, Jürgen. *The Crucified God.* London: SCM Press, 1974.

Munayer, Salim J., and Lisa Loden. *Through My Enemies' Eyes: Envisioning Reconciliation in Israel-Palestine.* Milton Keynes: Paternoster, 2013.

Murphy, Nancey. *Beyond Liberalism and Fundamentalism: How Modern and Postmodern Philosophy Set the Theological Agenda.* New York: Trinity Press International, 2007.

Nowell, David Z. *Dirty Faith: Bringing the Love of Christ to the Least of These.* Bloomington: Bethany House, 2014.

Perkins, William A. "Christian Youth in the Middle East." *The Ecumenical Review* 7, no. 4 (Jul 1955): 347–352.

Preuss, Horst Dietrich. *Old Testament Theology,* vol. 1. Old Testament Library. Louisville: Westminster John Knox Press, 1995.

Reisacher, Evelyne A., ed. *Toward Respectful Understanding and Witness among Muslims.* Pasadena: William Carey Library, 2012.

Richter, Julius. *A History of Protestant Missions in the Near East.* Edinburgh: Oliphant, Anderson & Ferrier, 1910.

Ryan, Curtis. "The New Arab Cold War and the Struggle for Syria." *Middle East Report* 262 (Spring 2012).

Salamah, Adib Naguib. "Evangelical Missions and Churches in the Middle East: Egypt and Sudan." In *Christianity: A History of the Middle East.* Beirut: MECC, 2005.

Stott, John R. W. "The Living God Is a Missionary God." In *Perspectives on the World Christian Movement,* edited by Ralph D. Winter and Steven C. Hawthorne, chapter 1. Pasadena: William Carey, 2009.

Stuart, Douglas K. *Exodus.* The New American Commentary, vol. 2. Nashville: Broadman, 2006.

Talman, Harley, and John J. Travis, eds. "Historical Development of the Insider Paradigm." In *Understanding Insider Movements: Disciples of Jesus within Diverse Religious Communities.* Pasadena: William Carey Library, 2016.

————, eds. "Muslim Followers of Jesus?" *Understanding Insider Movements: Disciples of Jesus within Diverse Religious Communities*. Pasadena: William Carey Library, 2016.

Tejirian, Eleanor H., and Reeva Spector Simon. *Conflict, Conquest, and Conversion*. New York: Columbia University Press, 2012.

United Nations Human Settlement Programme (UN-HABITAT). *Country Programme Document 2008–2009: Lebanon*. Nairobi: United Nations Human Settlement Programme (UN-HABITAT), 2008.

Warren, Rick. *The Purpose Driven Church: Growth without Compromising Your Mission*. Grand Rapids: Zondervan, 1995.

Watson, David, and Paul Watson. *Contagious Disciple Making: Leading Others on a Journey of Discovery*. Nashville: Thomas Nelson, 2014.

Winter, Ralph D., and Steven C. Hawthorne, eds. *Perspectives on the World Christian Movement*. Pasadena: William Carey Library, 2009.

Woodberry, J. Dudley. "Contextualization among Muslims: Reusing Common Pillars." In *The Word among Us: Contextualizing Theology for Mission Today*. Edited by Dean S. Gilliland, 282–311. Dallas: Word Books, 1989.

————. *From Seed to Fruit: Global Trends, Fruitful Practices, and Emerging Issues Among Muslims*. Pasadena: William Carey Library, 2011.

Wright, Christopher J. H. *The Mission of God's People: A Biblical Theology of the Church's Mission*. Grand Rapids: Zondervan, 2010.

Contributors

Martin Accad is the Chief Academic Officer of the Arab Baptist Theological Seminary (ABTS), Lebanon and Director of the Institute of Middle East Studies (IMES) located at ABTS. He is also Associate Professor of Islamic Studies, ABTS and Fuller Theological Seminary in Pasadena, California, USA. In addition, he is Director of Programs, Middle East for the Centre on Religion and Global Affairs (www.crga.org.uk). He wrote the missiological reflection in chapter 6.

Jonathan Andrews is British and lives in the UK. He has been researching and writing on the Middle East since 2003. His focus is on the issues that underlie the day-to-day lives of Middle Eastern Christian communities. He has a master's degree in Global Issues in Contemporary Mission from Redcliffe College, UK. He is the author of two books and the editor of a third (see bibliography) prior to editing this work.

Ashraf Bacheet is Egyptian. He has a degree in Pharmaceutical Sciences from Cairo University and a master's degree in Technology Entrepreneurship from University of Maryland. He manages the family business and has started and managed several businesses in the fields of advertising, media and publishing. He teaches Digital Media and Marketing at the Evangelical Theological Seminary in Cairo (ETSC). In 2010 he joined Christian Vision (CV) and launched the first ministry team solely focused on online evangelism in the Arab world. He is the Middle East Regional Director for CV. He wrote the missiological reflection in chapter 8.

Melanie Baggao was born in Southern California and now lives in Beirut. She is a Global Servant with American Baptist Churches International Ministries and is a Masters of Religion (MREL) student at the Arab Baptist Theological Seminary (ABTS). She wrote the background section of chapter 9.

Donnie Bentley is the director of the Alliance English Program in Beirut, Lebanon. He has lived in the Middle East since 2005. He wrote the background section of chapter 1 and co-authored the background section of chapter 2.

Rupen Das is Research Professor at Tyndale University College and Seminary in Toronto and the National Director of the Canadian Bible Society (CBS). Previously he had been on the faculty at ABTS and the director of the humanitarian programs of Lebanese Society for Educational and Social Development (LSESD). He has extensive global experience in relief and community development. Among his numerous publications is *Profiles of Poverty: The Human Face of Poverty in Lebanon* (Beirut: Dar Manhal al Hayat, 2011). For more, see his blog.[1] He wrote the whole of chapter 4.

Samah Fakhreldein was born and raised in Cairo, Egypt. She holds bachelors and masters degrees from ABTS. She moved to Brazil in 2017 together with her husband. She compiled the case studies in most chapters and wrote the background sections of chapters 5 and 8.

Ivan Fawzi is originally from Iraq, a former communist and atheist, born into a mixed Christian and Muslim family. He has lived in the former Czechoslovakia and Egypt. He has British nationality. At present, he lives with his wife and three children in Beirut and serves as the discipleship director in Resurrection Church, Beirut. He is the co-founder of al-Massira, an Arabic video-based resource for outreach and discipleship. He wrote the missiological reflection for chapter 3.

Nabil Habiby is a youth pastor who also works as a Dean of Students at the Nazarene School in Beirut. He is a lecturer in the New Testament at the Arab Nazarene Bible College and an adjunct faculty member and lecturer in the New Testament at ABTS. He is also a part-time doctoral student at the Nazarene Theological College in Manchester, UK, where he is doing research in evil spirits and impurity in Second Temple Judaism. He wrote the missiological reflection of chapter 9.

Robert Hamd is Lebanese and ethnically Druze. He has a doctorate in Intercultural Studies (DIS) from Fuller Theological Seminary, USA. In addition, he is ordained. He wrote the missiological reflection of chapter 5.

Brent Hamoud is American and has lived in Lebanon since 2007. He is involved in various faith-based initiatives and received a Master of Religion in Middle East and North African Studies from ABTS. He wrote the background section of chapter 6.

Chaden Hani is ethnically Druze and of Lebanese nationality. She is co-pastor of a Druze church. She holds a bachelor's degree in Theology from ABTS, a graduate of the MReL programme and is involved in formulating a

---

1. https://dascompassion.wordpress.com/rupen-das/ (accessed 11 December 2018).

theology to help Druze believers remain with their community. She is active in peacebuilding programmes through the "Church-Mosque Network" for the IMES. Internationally, she is involved in When Women Speak (www. whenwomenspeak.net). She wrote one of the case studies in chapter 10 and she and her husband feature in a case study in chapter 2.

Rabih Hasbany is Lebanese. Rabih was born and raised in Lebanon. He serves as the Lead Tutor for ABTS Online and General Editor for the Institute of Middle East Studies (IMES). He is studying in the IMES M-Rel program and writing his final paper on "Cross-cultural Model of Discipleship: A Way to Equip Syrian Followers of Christ to Lead Faith Communities in their Local Context." He wrote the missiological reflection in chapter 10.

Samar Khoury is Lebanese. She committed her life to Christ aged twenty. She did a course in Christian Apologetics that made quite an impact on her faith; she views her calling and passion as sharing the love of Christ with others. She has master's degrees in Theology and Psychology. She worked as a Bible teacher and a counsellor at a Christian school and was involved in discipleship, counselling and worship at her church. She moved to Germany in 2017 following her marriage to Tobias. She wrote the missiological reflection of chapter 1.

Suzie Lahoud is a second-year master's candidate at Harvard's Center for Middle Eastern Studies. She earned her bachelor's degree from Duke University graduating *magna cum laude* with a double major in Middle Eastern Studies and Russian. She additionally holds a Master of Religion in Middle Eastern and North African Studies from IMES. Suzie lived in Lebanon for seven years, the last four of which were spent working as a programme officer at MERATH, the relief and community development branch of the Lebanese Society for Educational and Social Development (LSESD). At this time, she managed projects responding to the urgent needs of refugees, internally displaced people and at-risk populations in Lebanon, Syria, and Iraq. Boston-born, Suzie grew up in Central Asia, and speaks fluent Russian and Arabic. She currently resides in Massachusetts with her husband of six years, Marvin Lahoud. She wrote the case studies in chapter 6.

Salim Munayer is ethnically Palestinian. He is founder and CEO of Musalaha, an organization working for reconciliation amongst Jews and Arabs/ Palestinians. He is the author or co-author of several books (see bibliography). He wrote the missiological reflection of chapter 7.

Chris Todd is from Alabama, USA. He moved to Lebanon in January 2012 and worked among Syrian refugees with the National Evangelical Council. During 2017 and 2018 they opened two schools for Syrian refugee children inside refugee camps near Tyre. Chris, together with his wife and four children, have seen the good news that Jesus is building his kingdom in the region. He wrote the background section of chapter 3.

Jesse Wheeler is American and lives in Lebanon where he is chief project officer for the Institute of Middle East Studies (IMES) and lectures on their Masters of Religion (MRel) programme. He wrote the background section of chapter 7.

Walid Zailaa is a faculty member of ABTS, teaching in the area of Old Testament, biblical languages and biblical theology, and also serves as the Leader of Academic Programs and Head Librarian. In 2007, he started his MDiv at ABTS, followed by an MTh at IBTS, and recently completed his DMin at Acadia. He wrote the missiological reflection in chapter 10 as well as one of the case studies.

Index

Institute of Middle East Studies
معهد دراسات الشرق الأوسط

The Institute of Middle East Studies Series provides academic theological books that are contextually appropriate to the MENA region and prophetically, sensitively and in a non-partisan manner inspire people and society. These resources represent the output of the Institute of Middle East Studies (IMES), founded by the Arab Baptist Theological Seminary, Beirut, Lebanon, which seeks to bring about positive transformation in thinking and practice between Christians and Muslims in the Middle East and beyond. The purpose of IMES is to increase general awareness about Middle East realities and to resource evangelicals to serve specific needs in the Arab World and among Arab communities.

Titles in this Series:

THE CHURCH IN DISORIENTING TIMES:
LEADING PROPHETICALLY THROUGH DIVERSITY

2018 | 9781783684342

THE MISSIOLOGY BEHIND THE STORY:
VOICES FROM THE ARAB WORLD

2019 | 9781783685981

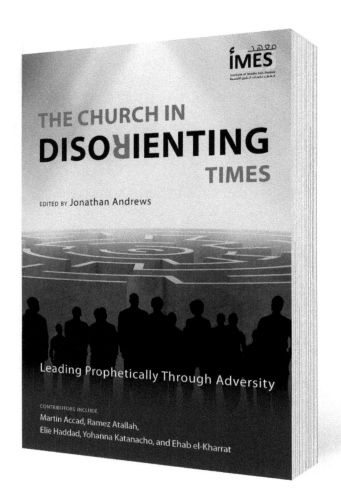

THE CHURCH IN DISORIENTING TIMES
LEADING PROPHETICALLY THROUGH DIVERSITY

Edited by Jonathan Andrews

9781783684342 | May 2018 | Paperback | 152 pages

Free international shipping on all orders

Email orders to literature@langham.org or call +44 1228 592033

Langham Literature and its imprints are a ministry of Langham Partnership.

Langham Partnership is a global fellowship working in pursuit of the vision God entrusted to its founder John Stott –

> *to facilitate the growth of the church in maturity and Christ-likeness through raising the standards of biblical preaching and teaching.*

Our vision is to see churches in the majority world equipped for mission and growing to maturity in Christ through the ministry of pastors and leaders who believe, teach and live by the Word of God.

Our mission is to strengthen the ministry of the Word of God through:
- nurturing national movements for biblical preaching
- fostering the creation and distribution of evangelical literature
- enhancing evangelical theological education

especially in countries where churches are under-resourced.

Our ministry

Langham Preaching partners with national leaders to nurture indigenous biblical preaching movements for pastors and lay preachers all around the world. With the support of a team of trainers from many countries, a multi-level programme of seminars provides practical training, and is followed by a programme for training local facilitators. Local preachers' groups and national and regional networks ensure continuity and ongoing development, seeking to build vigorous movements committed to Bible exposition.

Langham Literature provides majority world preachers, scholars and seminary libraries with evangelical books and electronic resources through publishing and distribution, grants and discounts. The programme also fosters the creation of indigenous evangelical books in many languages, through writer's grants, strengthening local evangelical publishing houses, and investment in major regional literature projects, such as one volume Bible commentaries like *The Africa Bible Commentary* and *The South Asia Bible Commentary*.

Langham Scholars provides financial support for evangelical doctoral students from the majority world so that, when they return home, they may train pastors and other Christian leaders with sound, biblical and theological teaching. This programme equips those who equip others. Langham Scholars also works in partnership with majority world seminaries in strengthening evangelical theological education. A growing number of Langham Scholars study in high quality doctoral programmes in the majority world itself. As well as teaching the next generation of pastors, graduated Langham Scholars exercise significant influence through their writing and leadership.

To learn more about Langham Partnership and the work we do visit **langham.org**